Japan Living

form and function at the cutting edge

MARCIA IWATATE AND GEETA K. MEHTA

PHOTOGRAPHY BY NACÁSA & PARTNERS

TUTTLE PUBLISHING
Tokyo • Rutland, Vermont • Singapore

Published by Tuttle Publishing, an imprint of Periplus Editions (HK) Ltd., with editorial offices at 364 Innovation Drive, North Clarendon, Vermont 05759 USA and 61 Tai Seng Avenue, #02-12, Singapore 534167.

ISBN 978 4 8053 0949 0

Distributed by:
North America, Latin America and Europe
Tuttle Publishing
364 Innovation Drive
North Clarendon, VT 05759-9436 U.S.A.
Tel: 1 (802) 773-8930; Fax: (802) 773-6993
info@tuttlepublishing.com
www.tuttlepublishing.com

Japan
Tuttle Publishing
Yaekari Building, 3rd Floor
5-4-12 Osaki; Shinagawa-ku; Tokyo 141 0032
Tel: (81) 03 5437-0171; Fax: (81) 03 5437-0755
tuttle-sales@gol.com

Asia Pacific
Berkeley Books Pte Ltd
61 Tai Seng Avenue
#02-12, Singapore 534167
Tel: (65) 6280-1330; Fax: (65) 6280 6290
inquiries@periplus.com.sg
www.periplus.com

Printed in Singapore

10 09 08   5 4 3 2 1

Author's note: We have adopted the Japanese way of presenting names in this book, with the family name first.

Front endpaper: Kamitaga Residence, pages 86–93

Back endpaper: Whole Earth Project, pages 156–161

Page 1: Wing Villa, pages 70–79

Page 2: Ring House, pages 94–99

Pages 4–5: Izumiya, pages 116–123

Pages 6–7: Kamitaga Residence, pages 86–93

CONTENTS

Design for a New Generation

All fine architectural values are human values, or else not valuable at all.

Frank Lloyd Wright, Architect

Left Horizon House is so named because it was designed to be a place to enjoy the horizon and the changing seascape throughout the year. Its living areas can be completely opened to the large deck, allowing the ambiance of the ocean to flow within.

Homes featured in this book are special places built as sanctuaries for the soul and places to dream in. They transcend functionality and resonate with human values of the owners and designers, working together as a team.

The homes in this book are also quintessentially Japanese, and represent a new burst in creativity in architecture and interior design seen over the past decade. The new designs are sharp, crisp, transparent and light. This is part of a worldwide excitement not felt at this scale since the Modern Movement at the dawn of the twentieth century. While generally this creative energy has been triggered by new materials, unprecedented prosperity, and environmental consciousness, it has a different emphasis in Japan. Here it is more intensely focused on form and space—historically the two strongest attributes of Japanese design. While working on this book we were often reminded of architect Arthur Erickson's saying, "Space has always been the spiritual dimension of architecture. It is not the physical statement of the structure so much as what it contains that moves us".

The sensitivity to high design in Japan goes deeper than in most other cultures, and is not limited to the rich and the stylish. It cuts across layers of society so that more people are willing to invest more in a sense of design than people in other countries are. The fact that about 20 percent of all high-design branded luxury products are sold in this small country illustrates this. Most houses in this book have been commissioned by young professionals, and most designs are by architects with relatively small ateliers. Architect is a "sensei" here, just like a doctor or a teacher, and a person to believe in rather than to question. Ban Shigeru, the architect of the new Georges Pompidou Center in Paris says that being an architect in Japan is more interesting because clients here are willing to single-mindedly push a design idea further than most clients are in the West.

While the new creativity in design worldwide is marked by the aesthetics of translucence, lightness and clean lines, Japan is the clear leader in these trends. Technologically advanced glass, metal coatings and joints, acrylics and paints allow fluid forms and transparency like never before. Meticulous detailing and workmanship achieved in these materials in Japan are abundantly cited elsewhere. The new materials lend themselves beautifully to Japanese aesthetics of subtle spatial definitions rather than overt and personality-driven design in the Western tradition. As in traditional Japan, construction details today are either exaggerated and made into an aesthetic system or eliminated altogether. Windows on many of the houses in this book are flush with the exterior walls, resulting in facades with a smooth appearance and a feeling of lightness. Walls and partitions made up of layers of large translucent glass panels appear dematerialized and magical. Tiny spaces look clean and expansive, just as they did in traditional Japanese architecture.

The houses in this book were selected for their innovative and inspiring designs, and we hope that our excitement about them comes through. While some homes in Tokyo have been included, most of them are away from Tokyo where land values still enable common people to build single-family homes. Many homes in this book are vacation homes built for people who already have a residence in the city, and want a second home for a peaceful

Above The clients wanted the exterior as well as interior of the Jogasaki Kaigan House to convey a sense of excitement about leaving the daily work routine behind. The architect chose to symbolize this concept via a large sculptural roof that mimics the contours of the site, which left wind flows and the natural topography of the site undisturbed.

Above More than a quiet retreat, the Manazuru Villa is a delightful mix of tactile interior finishes, forms and colors. The owners have filled their home with mid-twentieth-century Scandinavian furniture and contemporary art, which they are particularly fond of.

get-a-away. Not surprisingly, when interviewed, most of the architects said that the views and natural surroundings of the homes were their main inspiration for their design.

Most new Japanese architecture today is not as "green" in an environmentally sustainable way as traditional Japanese architecture was. It is indeed hard to beat the traditional Japanese house which was 100 percent recyclable and biodegradable. Even tatami mats were shredded and composted at the end of their useful life. Environmental ratings in Japan today are not as well developed as in Europe or USA. The fact that 20 percent of the housing stock in cities like Tokyo is torn down and rebuilt every year points to a hugely unsustainable—but lucrative building industry here. New earthquake laws and people's obsession with things new and fresh helps to perpetuate this. Only a short time after being completed, the houses in this book may be gone, torn down only to be rebuilt in the construction frenzy of Japan. Lovingly poured exposed concrete, the material of choice for stylish residences, is not treated as any more permanent than paper was in houses of yore. Beautiful does not mean big, expensive or permanent in Japan.

Most people in Japan today do not live in clutter-free and individualistic homes such as those featured in this book. They are the stuff of dreams for most of us. The majority opt for anonymity, which is synonymous with privacy in this crowded country. An average Japanese house is a private affair, and people seldom entertain at home. Children from a *danchi* or a large public housing project go to the same school, wear the same uniforms, and eat more or less the same things for dinner. Young mothers in danchi usually have a similar hairstyle and the wardrobe of a woman in her thirties—an age unanimously agreed upon by the Japanese women as the most desirable time warp to stay in. Mass-housing may produce team spirit, but can crush individuality. However, individuality cannot easily be designed or programmed into mass-housing. The ideal could be to make mass-housing more standardized and individualized at the same time, somewhat like Nike shoes today which are designed and produced by the cheapest labor and most expensive designers, and can be personalized with your name, color and signature if you want.

Of course Japan does have a tradition of individual expression in architecture. An invitation to rethink all concepts has been the central concept of Sukiya style architecture related to tea ceremony for hundreds of years. Houses presented in this book represent plenty of dreaming, creativity and self-expression that also are an important part of modern Japan. The personal idiosyncrasies of the F house (page 224), Manazuru Villa (page 20), Noborigama House (page 124), Izumiya (page 116) and Nakadai House (page 216) are reassuring. The sun-washed underside of the roof in The House in the Forest (page 162) redefines what roof and ceiling are, while a walk-in box that hangs out over the pitched roof reinvents the balcony. Homes of the future may morph to suit the needs and moods of the users, with walls that can change color, picture frames that can display a different Picasso on cue and music and aroma systems that can be programmed. Homes in movies like Star Wars and Minority Report present images of what future homes may look like, as do homes such as Horizon House (page 54), Hover House (page 232) and E House (page 246).

The countertrend to hyper-tech architecture in Japan is that people are also rediscovering their love of simplicity, natural materials, tatami mats and mud walls, somewhat like in the movie *Star Wars*, which included a hyper-tech senate hall, where Queen Amadea pleaded for help, and an adobe house, where Luke Skywalker grew up. Yatsugatake House (page 178), Sheet Metal Teahouse (page 140), Four-In-One House (page 200), Kamitaga Residence (page 86), Jogasaki Kaigan House (page 132) and Yamate House (page 170) all reflect a love for traditional materials. Three of the houses, Ring House (page 94), Yatsugatake House (page 178) and Whole Earth Project (page 156), also have a *doma*, the earthen-floored entrance hall typical of farmhouses of old Japan.

The Japanese housewife has been progressively outsourcing chores related to crafts, sewing, child care and cooking preparation to the eager businesses that strive to serve her ever more fully. Starbucks has even made it unfashionable to make coffee at home or the office. Convenience stores, called *conbini* in Japanese, are located closer to most homes in Japan than suburban sprawl would allow in North America. These stores are marvels of customer profiling and responsiveness. Here you can buy your meal or a snack suited to the time of the day and weather, use the ATM, order airline tickets or a package holiday, make prints or photocopies and pay your utility or tax bills, and tell them what else they can do to make your life more convenient. No place in Japan, from hiking trails to remote temples, is too far from a convenience store. This makes large food production or storage facilities in homes unnecessary, and helps to make a very small house quite comfortable. While it is now increasingly popular in Japan to import system kitchens from top of the line equipment makers like Gaggenau, many kitchens are used only for assembling preprocessed parts of a meal. Despite the proliferation of convenience stores and prepared foods, which serve the needs of mainstream Japan, many of the homeowners in this book have built single-homes to realize their own lifestyles, which in many cases include cooking, entertaining at home and gardening. This is particulary evident in the Niigata House (page 192), Manazuru Villa (page 20) and Nakadai House (page 216), as the owners are avid chefs.

Even very small houses can be inspiring sanctuaries for the soul, places to dream in, or to write an epic poem or two. A teahouse of yore in Japan was a place to get away, think deeply, and focus on a matter on hand, or to do "nothing," if you had reached that haloed level of being able to do so. In the fast-paced modern life in this crowded country, the only substitute to the teahouse available to most people regularly is the bathroom. It is no surprise that soaking in an *ofuro* is a national obsession, and a lot of design time and resources have been lavished on the bathrooms in the houses in this book. Even the luxurious houses in this book have just one or two bathrooms for the entire family, and an ofuro bath is still considered a cherished family place. These bathrooms are well appointed, and full of high-tech gadgetry. Wives who live in the newest homes may remotely start filling hot baths for their husband's return from work by using their cell phones. Roughly a third of all Japanese homes now have a Washlet toilet seat made by Toto, which includes a seat warmer, bidet and blow dryer, automatic seat sanitizers, and fragrance

Above The aesthetics system of the Noborigama House sets out to make a virtue of a
difficult building situation. While the walls on either end of the house have been finished
in white paint, the floors as well as ceilings have been made of wood. This system has been
consistently followed on all the levels, thus giving the entire house a sense of unity.

Above The feeling of an old Kyoto neighborhood is preserved in the limestone-floored patio of the Shimogamo Yakocho House through the use of smoked bamboo screens that allow the roofs of neighboring houses to be sensed but not clearly seen.

disposer, and costs between US $400 and $4,000. Matsushita Electric Co. sells toilets that can analyze urine for signs of diabetes, kidney disease and possibly even cancer. These toilets compile health records for the whole family, and major changes in urine composition can be automatically sent to your doctor. A sound muffler music box is another popular gadget installed to muffle embarrassing sounds. One can also order a prefabricated unit bath with all these features fitted in. The location, size and design of the bathroom in Horizon House (page 54), Ring House (page 94) and the Kamitaga Residence (page 86) of this book is a good example of the importance of a bath in a Japanese home.

A house is a place to put your belongings in. But why own things? In Japan this question is as old as Zen, which proposes that honest usage of material goods should involve true humility, justness and detachment. To consume or own any more than you need is a form of violence on our fragile planet. The need to own things is directly proportional to the insecurity, real or perceived, of not having them when you may need or want them. If you can get by without them, or have things available and affordable when you need them, there is no compulsion to own them. Authors Paul Hawken, Amory Lovins and L. Hunter Lovins in their book *Natural Capitalism* argue that ownership of things is an inefficient system from the point of view of environmental sustainability. People in Japan are experimenting with new forms of ownership of things, including homes. You do not need to own a car in Japan since the public transportation is so good. Leasing a car is another efficient alternative in a country where the value of cars, houses and most things drops sharply with age, and parking spaces are hard to get. Teenage Japanese girls, who are the most powerful consumer group in the world, often throw away their clothes after a season due to lack of storage space and unpredictability of next year's fashions. Clothing store Uniqlo has recently started taking back used clothing for recycling. Nakadai House featured (page 216) and Kamiyamacho House (page 64) in this book have very little storage, as the owners have perfected the art of not accumulating things.

When the Internet became ubiquities a few decades ago, people speculated that the death of distance might mean that people could now do the day's work from their laptops in their homes. While the concept of SOHO (small office home office) is catching on in Japan also and the powerful developer Mori is building some exclusive SOHO buildings in Tokyo, teleworking and telecommuting is unlikely to make major inroads in the lives of salarimen (coveted title of a salaried employee) in Japan. The tradition and comfort of teamwork and face-to-face camaraderie inculcated for centuries is still very strong here. Whole Earth Project (page 156), Tsurumi Atelier + Residence (page 100) and Atelier Semper (page 36) have been designed as integrated places to eat-work-play-sleep. Most of the people who currently work out of their homes in Japan are young and in the creative professions.

Nonelectronic memories are still important in some of the homes featured in this book. The living room windows in WS Residence (page 78) have been designed to frame a view of a cherry tree planted by the late mother of the owner, and her photograph has been placed facing that tree. The central column in Izumiya (page 116) is made up of the "hole" stone taken out from sculpture by Isamu Noguchi, a mentor of the owner-builder of this house.

Family and friends in Japan are increasingly connected (and perhaps also disconnected) by mobile phones. Desktops and laptop computers are considered too cumbersome, and the electronic industry is working hard to miniaturize functions of a computer into cell phones. About half the people in any subway car appear to be deeply engrossed in text messaging or photo sharing on their cell phones. This asynchronous communication is changing homes and families. It certainly offers more choices than sitting around a family dinner table listening to grandpa's tales that he forgot that he had already told you twice. Mothers whose children live away from home often send text messages to wake them up with electronic "Emotie" smiles. Like teenagers in the rest of the world, Japanese young people believe that if you are not on mixi.jp, the Japanese equivalent of a Facebook, you probably do not exist. These trends are reducing the need young people may feel to touch home base regularly. This is resulting in the opening of many new nomadic rest spots in public baths or manga-kissa Internet cafés for young people who come into Tokyo from the suburbs and float around the city for a few days without checking into a hotel.

Over half of homes in this book are for families where children have grown up and moved on, or extended families that do not have children. Japanese home industry and consumer goods manufacturers are gearing up to cater to the rapidly expanding "silver market" of aging people, many of whom live alone. Over 2,500 senior citizens in tea-loving Japan use a kettle called i-pot, which has been jointly developed by Zojirushi, Fujitsu and NTT. This gadget sends out daily usages-record emails to designated family members to assure them that aged parents are doing well enough to drink tea. According to editor-at-large and conservationist Kevin Kelly, "with more chip power than most computers, we should be seeing cars as chips with wheels, planes as chips with wings, and houses as chips with inhabitants." The result of the Japanese people's love of gadgets and their ability to pay for them is that a Japanese house is a clear winner in the race for the maximum number of remote control devices per capita. On the nonelectronic front, the popularity of the Chihuahua and 68 other varieties of toy dogs in Japanese pet shops is increasing with the aging population, to the extent that aromatherapy salons for dogs are featured in every new shopping center.

One of the major disappointments of the twentieth century has been the realization that the evolution of the human values has not kept pace with technological developments. Pervasive prosperity among one-sixth of the global population that lives in the developed world has proven that once people's basic needs are met, they do not necessary focus on beauty, truth, environmental and social justice or equitable development around the world. Instead, their additional resources are spent on ever more extreme forms of warfare, entertainment, and health issues related to overeating. This may be attributable to deft advertising and manipulation, but a human mind is sharper than that. Beauty of the homes in this book, and elsewhere, is perhaps simply a reminder of a higher purpose in life expected of us. When every thing is affordable and possible, what should one do?

Above This tearoom in the WS Residence combines Japanese traditions with innovative modernity. A wonderful example of this is the circular window cast into the concrete wall, which is a reference to *rikyu-mado*, the circular window favored by the sixteenth-century tea master Sen no Rikyu. At the center of the room, a kettle hangs over a soft coral stone fire pit from an industrial steel rod—an innovative interpretation of the traditional *ro* firepits.

MANAZURU
VILLA

More than a quiet retreat, this 330-square-meter weekend house is a delightful mix of tactile interior finishes, forms and colors. The owners are particularly fond of the mid-twentieth-century Scandinavian furniture and contemporary art, and have filled their home with these for their enjoyment. They looked at over twenty properties with architect Saitoh Yoshihiro of A-Study untill they found this site with a great ocean view located on a steep hill in Manazuru Peninsula, about one-and-a-half hour drive from Tokyo. Urban design guidelines regulating the exterior of properties here have resulted in a harmonious quality in this wooded oceanfront resort.

One of the architect's main concerns was the safety of the structure on this steep site. Pile foundations with reinforced retaining walls for moisture control and slope stabilization were used for the two lower floors. Special compact machinery that can be transported to deep mountain sites had to be deployed. The trapezoidal reinforced concrete columns at the lower floors have also been used as design features. Steel structure has been used for the top floor that houses the living areas. The house is entered from the third floor and steps down the steep site, so that every room enjoys a good ocean view.

The architect wanted to create a relationship between the house and the horizontal line of the ocean horizon. This was achieved by designing the staircase as the main axis of the house. From the staircase, one's line of sight is directed to the near edge of the negative-edge pool, which is lined up with the ocean horizon. The slightly lower farther side of this pool allows water to fall off its edge, bringing a sense of the eternal ocean into the house. This glass mosaic–tiled pool serves as a luxurious soaking pool by day and a dramatic lighting pool in the evening.

The architect sought to articulate the volumes of the exterior of the house in sturdy materials such as wood, stone and steel that could withstand the harsh ocean-side environment. Since he could not find stone of the desired texture within the project budget, custom-made tiles produced in Gifu Prefecture were used instead. For wet areas such as the bathroom and backboard of the kitchen counter, the tiles were finished with clear glaze and then fired a second time. Nonreflective materials were selected for the interior finishes to avoid reflections in the windows that would disturb the view of the ocean and its subtle color changes throughout the day. White plaster for the walls was mixed with touches of grey pigment. A nonglossy stain was used for the wood on the ceiling in the living room area. The house has been designed for a couple and their French miniature bulldog. The owner is an art dealer who chose lithographs by Andy Warhol, Frank Stella and others for the house. He and his wife are also avid collectors of vintage Scandinavian furniture and tableware. All of the furniture was brought in from Copenhagen.

The house is fitted with small luxuries and details that make this weekend retreat a truly fun experience. A high-end Linn Klimax audio system has been wired throughout the house and can be remote controlled from each room. The kitchen was designed by the wife who is an accomplished pastry chef. As with the design for the rest of her house, she wanted an eclectic vintage style for the kitchen. Instead of simply choosing an off-the-shelf kitchen system, she created her own design around a few vintage Scandinavian cabinets, a Gaggenau stove and an AEG dishwasher and oven unit. The Island counter has a marble inset for making pastry. Although each of these things is small in itself, together they create a whole that comforts the soul—the way only a good house can.

Previous spread The living room showcases the ocean view and the couple's extensive collection of vintage furniture. The PK22 rattan cane and steel chairs (circa 1955), PK61 glass and steel coffee table (circa 1955), PK31 leather sofa (circa1958) and PK33 stool (circa1958) are by the Danish designer Poul Kjaerholm. These original pieces have been manufactured by Ejvind Kold Christensen, a well-known furniture manufacturer. The sideboard with rattan doors was designed by Hans Wegner. A George Nelson bench sits by the window.

Above The raised living room floor is of limed white ash while the lower dining and kitchen area floors have been finished with slate tiles.

Left The Halyard lounge chair on the terrace was designed by Hans Wegner in 1950. Reclaimed stainless steel conveyor belts were used for the deck railing. The outer edge of a blue-tiled pool can be seen in the foreground.

Near right The bamboo-veneered vases were discovered by the owners on a trip to Ho Chi Minh City in Vietnam, along with vintage posters seen throughout the house. They have personalized their home with memories of their trips and of periods in history they are interested in.

Far right Sconce light fixtures in the stairwell were custom-designed by the architect. The wall washers set off the weathered texture of the unglazed tiled wall.

Left Vintage Knoll dining table and chairs are complemented by a pendant lighting fixture from Copenhagen. A necessary but obtrusive gadget, the TV has been recessed flush into the wall.

Right Reached via a sculptural wooden staircase, the loft above the dining area houses a small office.

Below The architect wanted to create a relationship between the house and the horizontal line of the ocean horizon. This dramatic stairwell, which serves as the central axis of the house, reminds residents of this relationship each time they go up and down it.

Below right The house, perched on its steep site, is entered from the third floor and steps down the site, so that every room enjoys a good ocean view.

Above (left to right) A yellow Swan Chair designed by Arne Jacobsen and an Andy Warhol "Brillo" lithograph brighten up a corner in the lower bedroom level. A soothing ocean view can be enjoyed at the bottom of the sweeping stairwell. The bathrooms are fitted with high-end fixtures from German manufacturer Grohe. Surfaced with blue glass mosaic tiles, the negative-edge pool parallels the ocean horizon, bringing a sense of the eternal ocean into the house.

Above Andy Warhol lithographs are hung on the north wall of the living room. The owner is a wine connoisseur and selected the grape series for that reason.

Left Instead of simply choosing an off-the-shelf kitchen system, the wife created her own design to complement the eclectic style of her house. The central features of the kitchen include the vintage Scandinavian cabinets, a Gaggenau stove, and an AEG dishwasher and oven unit. The wood and painted steel barstool was designed by Charlotte Perriand in the 1960s.

MOUNTAIN VILLA

Architect Ashihara Hiroko believes that a house should be designed as a "happiness holder." Besides a place to live, eat and sleep, it is a place to be with loved ones and a repository of memories and experiences. For this reason, the responsibility of an architect extends beyond designing spaces, colors and forms to also adding a spiritual and sensuous dimension to a home. The difference of experience between being in a space open to nature and that of being enclosed by insulated walls must be appreciated, and the perception of spaces in terms of movement, sight, sound and light also considered.

These principles are clearly reflected in The Mountain Villa, a 498-square-meter house designed by Ashihara Hiroko+Ashihara Hiroko Design Office. The 8,000-square-meter verdant site for this house has a grand view of Mount Asama in Karuizawa. A premier vacation resort area in Japan, Karuizawa is known for abundance of large trees, mountain views, sunshine and cool breezes. Based on his experiences of many beautiful resorts both outside and inside Japan, the owner encouraged the architect to take maximum advantage of these extraordinary surroundings in order to create an extraordinary but inviting villa, and to give physical form to the joy of living.

The boomerang-shaped home has been designed for a couple who enjoys entertaining. The building was placed in the middle of a site surrounded by big trees, which have been carefully preserved. To heighten the awareness of the mountain inside the house, the architect has situated the master bedroom wing of the house on an axis that connects it to the top of Mount Asama. Terraces and *engawa*-like transitional spaces help bring the experience of nature indoors.

To provide minimum obstructions to the views around the house, a light steel frame with 100-millimeter-diameter steel rod columns was chosen for its structural system. Due to the high humidity in Karuizawa, the steel frame rests on an enclosed spread-footing structure. A low-gradient roof has been designed so that snow and falling leaves can slide off easily. A hot water cleaning device has been installed to keep the skylight clear even during the winter months. Hebeschibe wooden frames were selected for their insulation qualities for the 3-meter-tall windows, which have been situated so as to avoid the sight of other buildings and to enhance the perception of the natural surroundings.

The house has been designed as a sequence of spatial experiences. Only the small entrance built in off-white textured French sandstone is visible from the approach through the northern gate. After entering the gate one walks down the porch beside a moss-covered courtyard full of rhododendrons and a circular reflective pool that lies half outside, but is visible through the low opening in the courtyard wall. The progression from the entrance to the inside of the house is accompanied by the gentle sound of water in this shallow dark steel pool. The entrance through this small enclosed area into the living space with very large windows dramatizes the natural landscape outside. A private living room is a few steps down from the main living room, which leads to the master bedroom. The kitchen and dining room are reached from the private living room, while each space has a generous terrace for outdoor living. Two guest rooms are located on the floor below.

Ash wood flooring has been used in the house for its distinctive color and wood grain, as well as for its ability to withstand floor heating and humidity. The floor heating was also designed for antifreezing effect on service pipes during the cold winters in Karuizawa.

Previous spread and above The architect refers to this villa as a "cozy cottage inserted into a grand space." Facing a large wooden deck, the living room is a stagelike setting for people to mingle and relax. Its 4-meter-tall ceiling, oversized sofas, sleek circular tables and light fixtures from the Italian manufacturer dePadova, give it a sense of expanded scale.

Left After entering the private back gate one enters a moss-covered courtyard full of rhododendrons and a reflective pool.

Near right The rattan chair on the terrace is from the Italian manufacturer Bonacina. This chair, as well as other furnishings in the villa, were handpicked by the architect for their timeless elegance.

Far right One of the guest bedroom suites of this expansive villa is tucked away in a private corner. A large chestnut tree provides shade to the terrace.

Left The tactile quality of plaster and cotton-fiber wall surfaces and wooden flooring underscore the care given to every detail of the house. This wall finish has the additional advantage of providing sound insulation.

Right The guest suites are located on the lower level of the wing that houses the private living room and master bedroom suite. The architect custom-designed a sculptural-like dresser for one of the suites (shown here in the open space across from the bed).

Below The open-plan master bedroom is seen from the double-sink vanity of the spa bathroom. The bathing area is located on the opposite side of this light-filled space with its own terrace.

Bottom To heighten awareness of Asama Mountain, all of the bedrooms, including the master bedroom suite seen here, have been placed on an axis connecting to the top of the mountain.

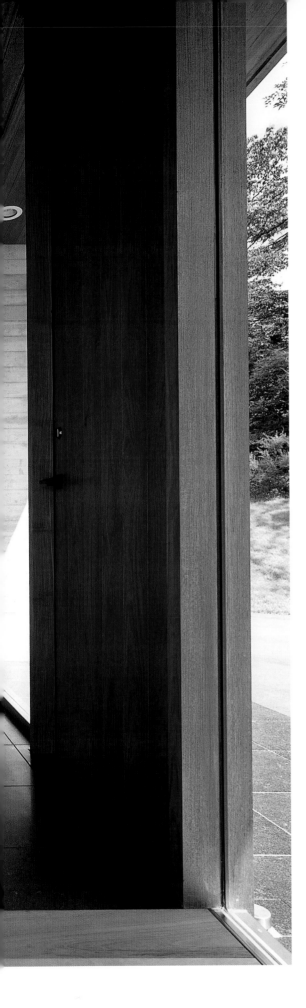

Far left top The architect designed this weekend villa as a "one night Shangri-la," to promote a sense of comfort, relaxation and well-being. This spirit is well illustrated in the open plan of all the bedroom suites appointed with luxurious spa bathrooms.

Far left bottom The hallway off the main entrance leading to the stairs to the lower level guest wing is enlivened with a delightful play of light. It is further accentuated by a narrow window at the end that artistically frames the greenery outside.

Left An elegant chair from the Italian Ceccotti collection is a sculptural as well as functional accent in the grand main entrance hall.

Below The small kitchen is located off the living room terrace that is equipped with a large charcoal grill. The couple enjoys alfresco entertainment during warm summer months on the terrace. Generous floor-to-ceiling closets to store the large collection of tableware used for entertaining flank the simple kitchen island. Large pendant lights from Italian collection Penta hang above.

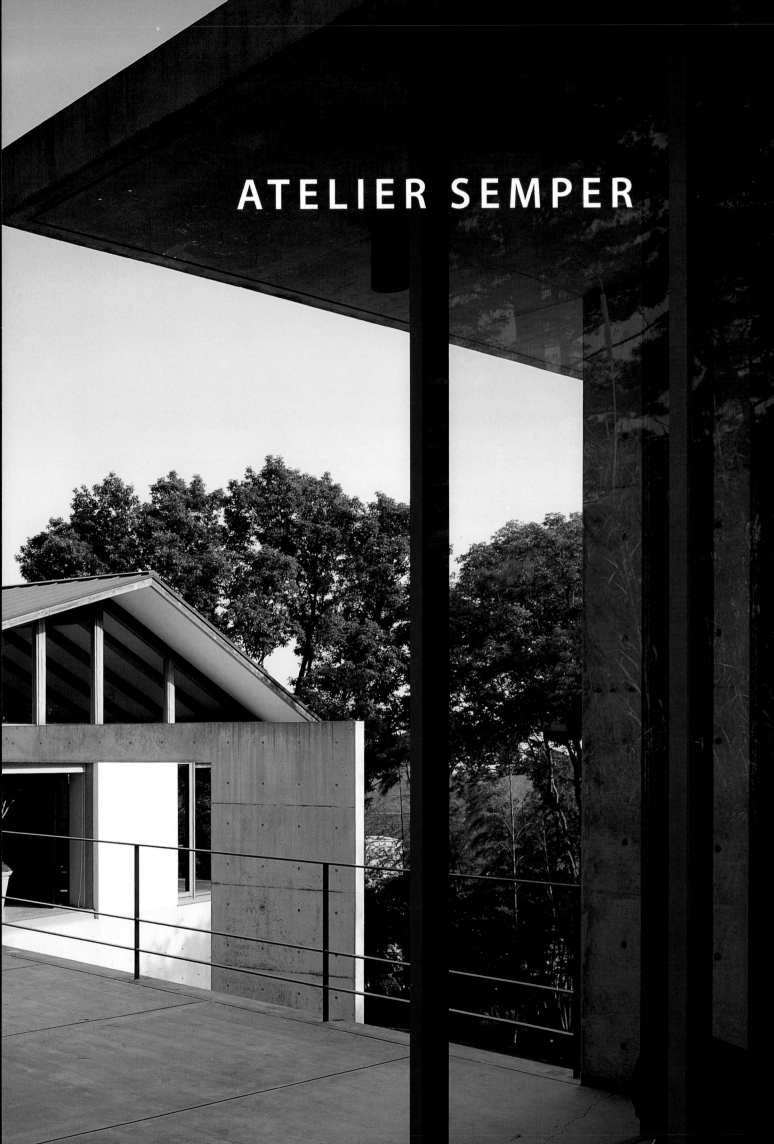

ATELIER SEMPER

This spectacular 600-square-meter weekend house + guesthouse + studio + gallery in the Okuike area of Ashiya district belongs to the well-known fashion designer Koshino Hiroko. Architect Kobayashi Hisashi +Kobayashi Hisashi Architect & Associates has done a very good job of interpreting his client's spirit of creativity and playfulness in her house. Koshino believes that it is important to get away from a crowded city like Tokyo to "reset" and heal one's mind amid nature. Originally from Kansai, she loves the Ashiya area and has spent her weekends here for the past ten years. Koshino believes that weekend retreats are the secret to her vitality, as many creative ideas as well as business opportunities have emerged in the middle of relaxed and warm human interactions.

The property is situated on a sunny 2530-square-meter site on the southern slope at the base of Mount Rokko in the Ashiya District. Away from the bustle of the big city, nature is at its best here in all four seasons. The site is located in a national park with extremely strict building regulations for environmental preservation. For example, the house was originally designed with a single large roofline, but the regulations necessitated breaking it up into smaller parts. These regulations also stipulate the minimum size of lots and the preservation of trees and topography. For all of these reasons, it is a particularly pleasant residential area even for Ashiya, a place known for luxurious homes. While many houses here vie with each other for their splendor, the client as well as the architect did not want the house to stand out like a large castle on top of the hill. They sought to create an understated retreat based upon its functional space program.

While it is usual to start the design process with an analysis of the site and functional program, this house was designed with the goal of creating a quality of timeless tranquility, using traditional Japanese concepts of beauty. Since abstracting the essence of Japanese design into contemporary fashion is the basis of her work, Koshino wanted the same for her house. This has been achieved with an uncluttered plan articulated with simple planes of exposed concrete walls and lack of fussy details.

Koshino also wanted to balance the private and public aspects of her life in the design of her house. Areas of pubic activity have been separated from Koshino's living quarters. The part of the property close to the entrance of the site consists of the gallery, the atelier, a library and stock rooms. Another part across from the dramatic swimming pool contains the salon and the private bedroom suites.

Various materials have been used in the hybrid structure of this house. The basement has been made of reinforced concrete to counter the lateral forces of the sloped site. A light wood truss has been used for the large span with the sloped roof needed for the salon. This is supported on a framework of slender steel pillars and beams. Large imported ceramic tiles have been used for flooring.

While summer is cool and comfortable in this area, winters are long and severe with the air temperature often dropping 5–6 degrees below that in the urban district that lies below the mountain. For this reason, floor heating has been provided in most living areas. Fireplaces and panel heaters supplement the floor heating where needed. An open fireplace has been installed in the center of the salon, attracting guests to gather around it.

Landscaping is an integral part of the experience of this house. The series of terraces, walkways and steps that form the transition from the public part of the property to the private part are as dramatic as the catwalks in the shows Koshino organizes, and enable the visitors to truly appreciate the natural beauty of Ashiya.

Previous spread Landscaping design has been designed as an integral part of the experience of this house. The series of terraces, walkways and steps form the transition from the public part of the property to the private part.

Above The sculpturesque wall that reaches across from the salon into the lozenge shaped pool also serves as diagonal structural bracing.

Right Surrounded by a luscious bamboo tree grove, a small sitting room for receiving business guests is built next to the atelier. It is tastefully furnished with Neoz seating designed by Philippe Stark for the Italian manufacturer Driade.

Left The grand salon is for personal relaxation and entertaining friends. A stylish mixture of sleek furnishings and antiques collected by the renowned fashion designer/owner sets the seductive tone.

Below far left A Japanese maple tree in the corner of the salon helps bring a sense of nature inside the house. The *sumi-e* (black ink brush) painting is by the owner.

Below near left The solid *bubinga* (African hardwood) timber bar counter faces the beautiful mountain view. The light fixtures installed above were designed by the German designer Ingo Maurer.

Right A baby grand piano sits in the corner of the grand salon against the backdrop of the national park.

Below This sitting room, built between the two guest bedrooms in the lower level of the private wing, has a grand view of the outdoors. The modular seating is designed by Emaf Progetti for Zanotta.

Above left Areas of pubic activity have been separated from Koshino's living quarters by this lozenge shaped pool that turns into a lighting pool at night. Above it is the grand salon with its light wood truss roof.

Above right The entrance gallery is an *engawa*-like space that runs along the length of the atelier. With floor to ceiling glass windows on one side, exposed concrete walls on the other, track lighting and tiled floor, it has a sense of Zenlike stillness.

Left Meticulous detailing has been carried throughout the house, including in the guest bathrooms in the lower level which are appointed with white marble and fittings from the German manufacturer Grohe.

Near right Located on the upper level of the atelier, the owner's office is flooded with natural light from the skylight streaming in through soft blinds. Her functional Poliform desk is paired with a Herman Miller chair while a striking red Alfa armchair from Zanotta provides for a few moments of relaxation.

Far right The custom-fitted bedding in the elegant guest bedroom is designed by the owner. Frank Lloyd Wright–designed Taliesin lamps provide bedside lighting.

Left Mannequins line the wall of the atelier. This functional open space buzzes with activity twice a year before the seasonal shows.

Below left A white leather sofa by Poltrauna Frau sits in front of the staircase leading to the guest quarters.

Right Two exotic dwarf trees and a mirror highlight the wonderful quality of space in the atelier.

Below Whimsical Maru Maru stools designed by architect Sejima Kazuyo from Driade line the gallery hung with *sumi-e* ink paintings by the owner. The atelier and staircase leading to the owner's office are seen through a doorway.

SHIMOGAMO
YAKOCHO
HOUSE

The Shimogamo Yakocho House, designed by Edward Suzuki+Edward Suzuki Associates, is a restful oasis in a Kyoto neighborhood. The 462-square-meter house has a sense of spaciousness unusual for a relatively small 360-square-meter corner lot. The owner's main request was that every room have a view of greenery. To achieve this goal, architect Suzuki drew on the traditional Japanese concepts such as the *shakkei* (borrowed scenery), *engawa* (peripheral transitional corridor between the inside and outside), *tsubo-niwa* (very small interior patio), *naka-niwa* (interior garden), *hisashi* (deep eaves) and *azumaya* (pavilion) to create a subtle relationship between the exterior and interior elements of the house.

The architect's reinterpretation of engawa and shakkei into a new concept of "interface" is of particular interest. The traditional engawa is both an exterior and interior space. In winter, the engawa separates the two, while in summer it fuses them. It is this blurred, fuzzy situation—that so typifies Japanese culture in terms of human-human as well as human-nature relationships—that the architect tried to replicate in the house. The practice of shakkei, or integrating the mountains and trees surrounding the site into the design, has been another important element of architecture and garden designs in Japan. These designs seek to contribute something positive to their environment. This wonderful give and take has now become difficult in increasingly crowded urban areas, and new buildings often put up walls or fences for protection from the chaotic surroundings. Suzuki's concept of "interface" seeks to create a transitional space between the crowded neighborhood and the interior, with the goal of editing out the visual chaos while still allowing daylight and breezes to enter the inner space. This interface, made of a peripheral screen and greenery, acts as a buffer zone between the inside and outside of the building. At night, the house sheds warm light on the neighborhood in a spirit of give and take typical of traditional Japanese architecture.

Two types of interface screens have been used in this house. One is the circular, frosted-glass screen that envelopes the northeastern part of the second floor and roof and is located above the main entrance. Reminiscent of the traditional Japanese paper shoji screens, this translucent screen allows in abundant, soft, natural light while rendering the terrace completely private. The other "interface" is the vertical smoked bamboo screen, which allows the roofs of neighboring houses to be "sensed" but not clearly "seen." Inside this screen is a buffer of greenery, consisting of tall bamboos, low shrubs and wild grasses typical of Kyoto. This interface provides a good measure of privacy to the open patio on the second floor.

The plan of this house is elegantly composed of a perfect square, with a grid of nine smaller squares of 5400 millimeters inside. The original, large square has been overlaid with an arc of the circular frosted-glass screen on the second floor and roof. The basement is comprised of a sunken courtyard around which a Japanese room, family room, guest room and ancillary areas have been arranged. The first floor is comprised of the entrance foyer, two bedrooms with ensuite bathrooms. The second floor boasts a 3-meter-high ceiling, and houses the living, dining and kitchen area within one large space. The roof terrace boasts a special moon-viewing platform and pergola.

Three-dimensional models of the house were made so that every aspect of the interior could be carefully thought out. The architect was charged with selecting all furniture, furnishings and equipment. The washbasins, created by four different artisans using different media for each one of the four bathrooms, are an example of the innovative ideas the architect brought to this task.

Vernacular materials have been used throughout the house to bring the spirit of traditional Japanese architecture into this contemporary setting. Bamboo has been used on the floors, doors, furniture and screens. Limestone has been used on the exterior as well as interior floors and walls. Japanese plaster and paper has been used for interior walls, ceilings and partitions. Real autumn grass, a plant very dear to Japanese people, has been embedded into the finish on the sliding doors in the Japanese room.

Previous spread The feeling of an old Kyoto neighborhood is preserved in the contemporary limestone-floored second floor patio through the use of smoked bamboo screens that allow the roofs of neighboring houses to be "sensed" but not clearly "seen." Minimalist aluminum frame and teak furniture are by Belgian manufacturer Extremis.

Above A circular screen made of dot-point double-tempered frosted glass masks the facade of the house. The approach is paved with bush-hammered rusted granite that is interspersed with squares of mondo grass, *tokusa* (scouring rush) and bamboo trees, plants that are typical of Kyoto gardens.

Left Real autumn grass called *susuki*—a plant very dear to Japanese people—has been embedded into the plaster finish and the *washi* paper on the sliding doors in the Japanese room. A handwoven bamboo floor lamp casts intriguing shadows.

Above A contemporary *ro* (fire pit) with a sculptural steel chimney divides the living area from the dining area and the kitchen. Bamboo trunk accents and wooden slatted screens bring a touch of outdoors to this space.

Left The master bedroom is a private, yet airy space with a view of the bamboo trees planted in the courtyard below. Bedside light fixtures have been built into the piece of furniture that also acts as a headboard.

Above right Soft textures and shades of white define this living room. The Sona sofa is by Arflex. The coffee table seen here, as well as all other tables in the house, have been custom designed in bamboo parquet.

Right To complement the bamboo parquet dining table, architect Suzuki selected Flo wicker chairs designed by Patricia Urquiola for Italian manufacturer Driade.

Right In the spirit of *tsukimidai* (moon viewing platforms) of the ancient Japanese aristocratic villas, the rooftop terrace has a striking panorama of the surrounding hills of Kyoto. The wood deck, benches and the pergola have been made of *garapeira*, a Brazilian hardwood.

Below The architect selected different materials for the floors of the three-tiered open spaces to give each area its own identity—limestone, Brazilian hardwood and bush-hammered rusted granite paving.

Right (clockwise from top left) Subtle combinations and natural textures have been celebrated throughout this house. Bamboo trees cast delicate shadows on the hand-troweled limestone and aggregate plaster wall in the lower courtyard. A contemporary *ro* (fire pit) provides a gathering place for the family sitting on the floor in traditional Japanese style. The rattan easy chair designed by Patricia Urquiola is set against the hand-troweled plaster and bush-hammered rusted granite paving, inviting residents to take a relaxing pause from their busy lives. A pair of incense burners sit on the Corian slab shelf in the master bathroom.

HORIZON HOUSE

Designed by Ogawa Shinichi+Ogawa Shinichi & Associates, the 461-square-meter Horizon House in Atami city sits atop a 40-meter-steep cliff that rises from the Atami Bay in the Pacific Ocean. This unique location gives this house a spectacular view without any man-made distractions. This area, as well as the famous resort town of Atami nearby, is known for therapeutic hot springs.

The Horizon House has been so named as the couple who own it wanted a place to enjoy the horizon and changing seascape throughout the year. A large outdoor space that could be integrated with the living areas was also part of the program for this house. In response, Architect Ogawa designed the house on two levels that allows the ambiance of the ocean to flow within. The first floor is made of reinforced concrete in the shape of a box culvert, and includes the bedrooms, a tatami-matted room and ancillary areas. The bedrooms face the ocean while the ancillary areas back into the cliff. The garage entrance is also built at this level.

A steel structure was selected for the second floor to allow the ocean facade of the living spaces to be completely glazed and open to views without the visual interruption of columns. Full-height glass doors along this entire facade slide open to connect the living areas to an expansive terrace outside to bring the ocean breeze and sound into the house.

The architect designed automated aluminum shutters to protect the house and the large expanse of glass during the owner's absence and typhoon storms. The110-square-meter living/dining and kitchen space and a large Japanese style *ofuro* bath have been conceived as part of one continuous experience, with the main entrance also located at this level.

The luxurious ofuro in this house underscores the importance given in Japan to the ritual of bathing. The social and spiritual dimensions attached to this ritual are comparable to those accorded to a sauna in Northern Europe. People wash outside before entering the hot soaking tub that is designed to stay hot for the long duration of soaking. In the past such baths were heated by firewood from below, whereas electric heaters fill that need in contemporary baths. Although traditional public bathhouses are fast disappearing, they were an integral part of the neighborhoods and downtowns in the past and are prominently featured in woodblock prints and literature. An increasing number of people now have private ofuros in their homes, while the popularity of the modern "super-ofuros" as places of relaxation and amusement also continues to rise. The sublime bathroom in the Horizon House has a 2.4-x-1.2-meter soaking bathtub sunken into the floor. Both are surfaced with simulated marble that resists staining from the sulfur-rich hot spring water that is piped into the house. The full-height glass wall on the ocean side creates a feeling of bathing in the ocean.

Previous spread Full-height glass doors slide open to connect the living areas to an expansive terrace outside to bring the ocean breeze and sound into the house. The 110-square-meter living/dining and kitchen space and a large Japanese style ofuro bath have been conceived of as part of one continuous experience, with the main entrance also located at this level.

Above and left The capacious modular sofa from Italian manufacturer Natuzzi offers a comfortable place for napping, snacking, TV viewing and the large number of guests that frequent the house.

Right An oversized pine wood dining table designed by the architect sits in front of the low Corian-surfaced wall with the kitchen behind it. The classic soap-finished beech wood "Wishbone" chairs designed by Hans Wegner complement the mood.

Left Situated atop a 40-meter-steep cliff that rises from the Atami Bay in the Pacific Ocean, the unique location gives the house a spectacular ocean view uninterrupted by any man-made distractions.

Below The Miura Peninsula can be seen in the distance to the left in the wide-open seascape view from the Horizon House.

Top The entire inside wall of the living and dining areas has been designed with floor-to-ceiling built-in storage to reduce clutter and thus help preserve the integrity of the architecture. Four of the doors among the long succession of doors on this wall lead to rooms tucked away from the great room—a powder room, pantry, study and utility room.

Middle The architect designed the automated aluminum shutters to protect the house and the large expanse of glass during the owner's absence and typhoon storms. This is an innovative interpretation of the wooden storm shutters that protected shoji screen doors in traditional Japanese architecture.

Above The terrace is surfaced with high-gloss simulated marble tiles for easy maintenance and the added attraction of reflecting the blue skies.

Far left top The staircase leading to the lower level bedrooms is illuminated with natural light flooding down from the living room.

Far left bottom Each detail of the house has been kept stubbornly clutter free.

Left A low splashboard behind the kitchen counter and sink is all that is needed to separate the kitchen space from the living room.

Below A corridor of white walls, floor and ceiling is set off by just a few pieces of artwork and pottery.

Top The 2.4-x-1.2-meter soaking bathtub in this ofuro has been sunk into the floor so as not to break the line of site toward the ocean. The bathtub as well as the floor is made of simulated marble.

Below The bedrooms on the lower floor as well as the living areas on the top floor enjoy uninterrupted ocean views.

Right All the furnishings in the house have been chosen for their lightness and clean lines so as not to distract from the ocean view.

Below The lower floor that houses the guest rooms has been constructed as a concrete culvert, while a lighter steel structure was used for the floor above.

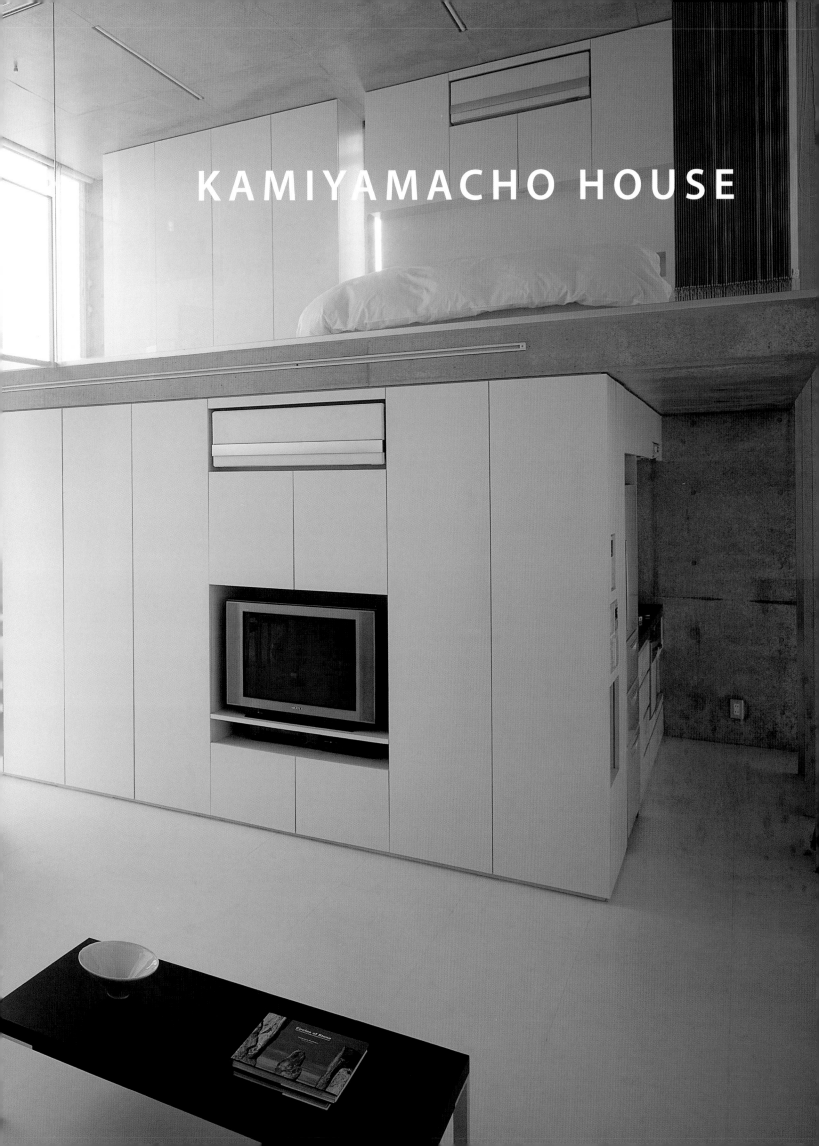

KAMIYAMACHO HOUSE

This 82-square-meter house is located in a densely populated residential area of Funabashi City in Chiba Prefecture—with haphazard growth of small detached buildings that is typical in the suburbs of Tokyo. The challenge of designing on small lots in such areas is compounded by the strict zoning laws relating to sunshade restriction.

The program requirements of comfort and privacy for a young couple have been accommodated on this small site to create spaces that are fun and inspiring. Having designed many houses in such neighborhoods, architect Fuse Shigeru of Fuse Atelier has learned to deal with such constricting circumstances with flair. All the houses designed by him have immaculate detailing and clean volumes, so that even small interior spaces and small surface areas on the exterior have a feeling of expansiveness.

The exterior of this small house is a simple flat box of concrete measuring 6.3 (height) x 9 (width) × 5.4 (depth) meters. Two sides of this box are made entirely of glass curtain walls. Frosted glass has been used in the curtain walls for privacy in this neighborhood where the houses are built very close together, with only a 50-centimeter setback required from the lot lines. At night the curtain wall glows with dispersed light like a lantern. This envelope is punctuated only with one deep aluminum canopy at the entrance.

The spacious feeling inside the house belies its small size. Space from the double-height living room flows past a clear glass wall into the bedroom built on a mezzanine. The centerpiece of the living space is a grand piano for the wife who is a pianist. The mezzanine located at a height of 4.5 meters is reached by a crisp white spiral staircase, which continues up to the roof terrace. The entrance lobby, kitchen, and bathroom have been placed underneath the mezzanine. The roof terrace is surrounded by 1.8-meter-tall walls and is open only to the sky to provide privacy from the neighbors. These boundary walls also act as structural beams for the sides with curtain walls. The terrace floor has been designed to be filled with water to become a shallow pool to reflect the changing clouds, sunlight and wind.

Previous spread Furniture and storage have been built-in where possible to help avoid clutter in this small house. The Zen cliché of "elimination of the inessential" is an essential part of the design strategy of this house.

Above Frosted glass has been used in the curtain walls for privacy in this neighborhood where the houses are built very close together, with only a 50-centimeter setback required from the lot lines. At night this curtain wall glows with dispersed light like a lantern.

Right The centerpiece of the living space is a grand piano for the wife who is a pianist.

Above The mezzanine bedroom located at a height of 4.5 meters is reached by a crisp white spiral staircase, which continues up to the roof terrace.

Right The clear glass wall between the living room and the bedroom helps make both spaces appear spacious, while still allowing for sound privacy.

Above The roof terrace is filled with water to become a shallow pool to reflect the changing clouds, sunlight and wind.

Below left A single slab has been inserted into the side of the building to provide shelter for the entrance as well as the parking space. It is this sort of immaculate detailing that results in the minimal aesthetics of this house.

Below right In keeping with the clutter-free aesthetics of the rest of the house, the air conditioning unit in the bedroom has been fitted into the partition wall that separates the walk-in closet.

WING VILLA

Designed by Utsumi Tomoyuki+Milligram Architectural Studio, the Wing Villa gets its name from its large angular roof that sweeps over the house and seems ready to take flight. This large roof culminates in a deep overhang that slants upward on the north to mark the entrance, and is reminiscent of the overhanging eaves of traditional temples in Japan. The roof integrates an irregular innovative plan that is a result of the desire to save as many trees on the site as possible, and to create the best possible views for the house. This wing imagery is further reinforced by the shape of the western side of the house that has been lifted off the ground to leave the tree roots undamaged, with its underside tapered upward.

This 260-square-meter house in Karuizawa, Nagano Prefecture has been situated on the northern part of a 3300-square-meter wooded site. The land slopes eight meters down from the northern entrance toward the south. Although it is a single storied house, this level difference on the site gives the living areas a feeling of being on the upper level, with abundant sunshine, breeze and views of the nearby trees and distant mountains toward the south.

The complex program and plan of this vacation house designed for a family of four benefited from the relationship of trust between the client and architect, who also helped in the site selection process. The plan has been organized along the north-south axis in the shape of a Japanese fan, starting from the entrance point and spreading out toward the south. The gallery-like views from the large windows on the south are seen across the long corridor from the entrance, with several level changes enroute. This north-south axis, along which most public areas have been arranged, has been intercepted in the middle of the house with an east-west corridor axis, along which private areas such as the bedrooms and guest room have been located.

The structure consists of thin concrete load-bearing walls with diagonal metal bracing. Many of these walls have been placed at an angle which, along with the sloping surfaces of the furniture, makes the experience of the house special. Exposed concrete and stone on selected walls and floors have been used as accents in the otherwise white plastered walls of the living areas. The rough texture of these surfaces is articulated with wall washer lights and contrasts well with the glossy paint on the white walls elsewhere in the house.

Previous spread The curved shape of the storage area on the lower level and projecting balconies of the living areas above give the southern elevation of the house a shiplike appearance.

Opposite Limestone has been used for the floors in the entrance hall and fireplace room. The living and dining areas are seen in the background.

Below The dining table consists of a slab of *sakura* (Japanese cherry) wood resting on custom cast-iron legs. It is complemented with banker's chairs. The large mullionless glass wall opens up the room to the views outside.

Above The large custom-built island kitchen counter is surfaced with walnut wood veneer and a stainless steel countertop.

Top left The bed, desk and shelves in the master bedroom have been designed by the architect using *tamo* wood.

Left The lighting design makes this house particularly dramatic at night. Cove lighting from the ceiling and alcoves has been used throughout the house. Strips of accent lighting along the staircase floor add to the effect.

Right Inclined walls and sloping surfaces of the furniture add to the delights of the house, as seen in the Japanese room located at the tip of one "wing."

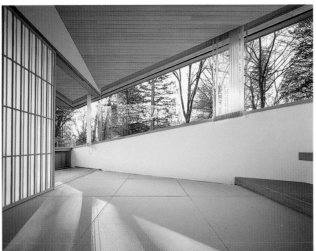

Left The use of a blonde wood finish on the ceiling throughout the house and on the underside of the large overhangs give the house a sense of integrity. Fanlights wash the ceiling with light, making them appear taller than they are.

Right Surfaced entirely in black matte tiles, the guest bathroom is equipped with a chrome towel heater from PS Heating Systems, a nice amenity for the cold winters of this area. The sink has been designed by Phillipe Starck for Duravit.

Below A Uno di Noi sofa designed by Sergio Brioschi and a Lits side table, both from Arflex, sit in front of the sand stone masonry wall in the living room.

Below right One whole wall of the master bathroom has been glazed to provide a luxurious view of the trees outside. In contrast to the dark guest bathroom, this spa bathroom is surfaced with white tiles and fitted with a circular Avelco Jacuzzi.

WS RESIDENCE

Kagoshima city, the capital of Kagoshima Prefecture, is located on the southwest tip of Kyushu Island and is known for its warm and humid climate, abundant water, rice paddies and frequent typhoons during summer months. The suburb of Wada-cho, where this house is located, has historically been a desirable neighborhood due to the good quality of its water that came from the nearby Jigan Temple. The level of the site lies 1.2 meters above the street level, and was probably raised at some point in the past to protect against the frequent floods in Kagoshima. The owner wanted to have his new house on this 483-square-meter lot designed to recall the special features and memories of his old ancestral bungalow that had previously stood at this site.

The owner, a dentist with a keen appreciation for architecture, spent over ten years studying the work of various architects in Japan before inviting Nakahara Yuji +Nakahara Yuji Architect Design Office to design this 270-square-meter house for him and his wife, their daughter and his father. The architect worked closely with the owner in realizing the complex program and responding to the site conditions.

The facade, the sloped approach path, and the two-car garage form a sculpturesque composition seen from the street. The gentle slope leading up to the entrance was designed at the owner's request to create a physical as well as emotional transition before entering the gate. This concept is reminiscent of the meandering *roji* paths in traditional stroll gardens that prepare the guest for entering the "inner world of tea." This is not surprising given that the owner is a practitioner of the "way of tea." After crossing the sliding latticed entrance gate made of *sugi* wood, one is led via a bridge over a water garden to enter a hallway that leads to an exquisite tea room on the left and the entrance to the rest of the house. The architect interpreted traditional elements of the tea room using new materials and modern design. A wonderful example of this is the circular window cast into the concrete wall, which is a reference to Rikyu-mado, the circular window favored by the sixteenth-century tea master Sen no Rikyu. Other innovative features include the kettle hung from an industrial steel rod over a soft coral stone fire pit in the center of the room, the entrance *fusuma* sliding door surfaced with copper sheets, and the dark-stained latticed screen doors that swing inward to fully open the tearoom to the water garden outside.

The house consists of two rectangular blocks placed at right angles to each other. Landscaped areas, visible from the large glass windows, blur the border between inside and outside of this horizontal geometric structure. The space in the living room, which has a 5.5-meter-high ceiling, is further enhanced by sinking the limestone floor by 600 millimeters. This was also done to afford a good view of an old Someiyoshino cherry tree that the owner's late mother had planted so that her family could enjoy the annual *hanami* (cherry blossom viewing) at home. Her photograph faces the tree.

Unlike many architects, Nakahara gets deeply involved in the landscaping for each house he designs. He has worked with the same gardener for other houses, such as K Courtyard House featured in this book, to ensure that trees and plants complement the architecture. The result is a well-designed garden with a carpet of moss and mature trees including maple, *sakura* (Japanese cherry) and hydrangea. The garden, which is visible from the two long glass-walled sides of the house, also provides privacy.

The thin-walled reinforced concrete frame structure of the house has been supplemented by six concrete-filled steel pipe columns (140 millimeters in diameter, 8 millimeters thick) to attain a clear span of ten meters along its width. Besides the architectural program, the architect's overriding concern was to provide sufficient air circulation in the house to counter the heat and humidity of summers in Kagoshima, and to design protective measures against frequent typhoons. These concerns were met by using louvered glass for windows to bring in natural breezes, and by wooden storm shutters along all the glass windows. Floor heating and lighting fixtures have been integrated in the floor slabs to add to the comfort of this special home.

Previous spread A wonderful view of treetops can be seen from the windows of the second floor family room. A Le Corbusier–inspired glass desk sits in the study a few steps up from the family room.

Above The owner purchased the *sashimono* (traditional tongue and groove) *andon* lantern designed by the popular lacquer artisan Akagi Akito many years ago in anticipation of this tearoom, which has been intepreted by the architect with new materials and a modern design sensibility.

Above and right The owner himself lovingly selected each piece of furniture and tableware for his new residence. The white leather Piero Lissoni box sofa in the living room has been manufactured by Living Divani and Ixc. The nara wood coffee table was custom built for this room. The architectural model of the house sits atop the built-in credenza.

Left The natural rock in the entrance was found by the furniture makers who thought that it would match perfectly with the spirit of this house. It not only acts as a shelf to hold flower arrangements but also as a perch to sit on for putting on and removing shoes at the entrance, as is the custom in Japan.

Below Piero Lissoni's box sofa from Living Divani and Ixc adds to the ambience provided by the fireplace, which was custom built in steel and soft coral stone.

Top left and right From the sliding latticed entrance gate made of sugi wood, one is led across a bridge to the entrance hall. Concrete flooring with metallic trowel finish and wax coating is used for the decks, stairs and entrance hall. The walls and ceilings are in exposed concrete finish.

Above The dining table, custom built in nara wood, and the white leather chairs from Time & Style form a harmonious complement to the wooden floor. The kitchen is enclosed in the concrete walls.

Above The architect's interpretation of this tearoom resulted in an exquisite example of modern design with innovative use of new materials. A wonderful example of this is the circular window cast into the concrete wall, which is a reference to *rikyu-mado*, the circular window favored by the sixteenth-century tea master Sen no Rikyu, and the industrial steel rod on which the kettle hangs over a soft coral stone fire pit in the center of the room.

KAMITAGA RESIDENCE

A few hours along the coast from Tokyo, Atami is a famed resort town known for its hot springs and honeymooners during the fifties, and *Omiya no Matsu*, the pine tree under which two lovers parted in a popular novel *Konjikiyasha*. The owner chose to build his post-retirement home on an oceanfront property on the outskirts of this town to pursue his hobby of scuba diving. The process of site selection, design and construction of the house took ten years, but the owner considers this project one of the greatest achievements of his life, and well worth the time it took. Although a much larger house had been envisaged in the beginning, its size was reduced to 195 square meters over time due to a combination of a fixed budget and the insistence of the owner and the architect on the highest quality materials and finishes.

The architect Watanabe Akira+Watanabe Akira Architect and Associates and the owner like contemporary design that reflects the Japanese philosophy of "elimination of the inessential." The owner also wanted clean modern spaces to showcase his art and antique collection. The other key concept in this house is the expression of horizontality, in contrast to the verticality that is predominant in cities. The house has been designed with its southern face open to ocean views while its northern facade facing the mountain is closed in by a slanting exposed concrete wall. The angle of this wall's slope mirrors that of the mountain.

The stretches of the concrete retaining walls and the green *oka* bamboo grass field seen from the approach road that climbs up the mountain create a perfect preamble to the horizontal profile of this house. The entrance to this house, designed for a couple and their eleven-year-old son, is accessed via a bridge over the sloping bamboo grass field. Crossing over this bridge into the house, the feeling changes entirely as the ocean toward the south comes into view. The sliding doors along the entire wall on this side can be opened to panoramic view of the pine trees, blue sky and the indigo-colored ocean without the interruptions of any window mullions.

The *engawa*-like patio off the living room acts as the transitional space between the interior and exterior of the house. The two-and-a-half-meter-deep roof overhang and the cantilevered floor of this patio further narrow the aperture of the ocean view, adding to the feeling of horizontality. Teak, a premier hard wood from the monsoon forests of South and Southeast Asia, has been used for the floor and ceiling of this patio. The natural oil in this wood makes it weather resistant and good for structural as well as outdoor use. The combination of texture and quality of lines achieved with teak wood and exposed concrete in this house is a work of art in itself.

The living room is devoid of any furniture. Seating has been provided in a sunken area with leather cushions, facing the custom-built fireplace. The *hanchiku* earthen wall in the living room is a special feature that the architect is very fond of. It is built using an ancient technique that originates from China in which layers of earth are applied on framed wooden boards. Such walls have been used as load-bearing walls in several ancient world heritage sites such as Horyuji Temple in Japan and the Great Wall of China. Earthen walls possess a naturally dehumidifying effect and are very suitable for the hot and humid summers in Atami.

Air conditioning has been designed so that the outlets are in the floor rather than in the ceiling, with the plenum between the structure and the flooring acting as duct space. This efficient system heats and cools only the immediate space around the occupants and it eliminates drafts. Further, cooled air in summer and warmed air in winter is fed back into the plenum, further reducing air conditioning loads.

The large inter-related planes of this house are echoed in its landscaping concept. A series of retaining walls, walkways, a viewing platform and rocks punctuate the field of bamboo grass over the gently sloping hills. A walkway from the ocean provides a place of rest for the family on its way back home from scuba diving. It leads to the backdoor where wet diving clothes can be changed before entering the house.

Above and previous spread The sliding glass doors have been covered with reeds in the fashion of *sudo*, the traditional shades used in Japan during summer. When these glass doors are closed, the view seen through the silhouetted reeds appears like a Japanese folding screen painting.

Left Avoiding vertical interruptions to the flow of space has resulted in an uncluttered interior. The dining area has been designed in a sunken pit so that the top of the table is at the same level as the floor. The custom-built table has a built-in charcoal pit for boiling water and grilling food. The window has been squeezed to a narrow slit at the bottom of the wall, to provide just a glimpse of the bamboo grass field outside. This is reminiscent of *yukimi-mado* windows of traditional teahouses, designed to focus the view from the interior on fresh snow on the ground while cutting off the view of the street or other distractions.

Right The exterior as well as the interior of the house is composed of large uninterrupted exposed concrete, clay, and teak wood surfaces. The concrete is beautifully imprinted with the pattern of cedar wood framework used in its casting process.

Below An antique stone water basin sits like an exclamation mark in the field of native bamboo grass shrubs, which are easy to maintain.

Left The architectural composition of large inter-related planes of this house is echoed in its landscaping concept. A series of concrete retaining walls, walkways, a viewing platform and rocks punctuate the field of bamboo grass over the gently sloping hills.

Below left Water lilies bloom in a stone tsukubai under the hot summer sun.

Below right A *sekimori-ishi* stone, tied with bracken rope to indicate its special status, is normally found in traditional tea gardens placed atop a stepping stone indicating a route that should not be taken. Here, it indicates that the owners are not at home.

Right Soaking in an outdoor *ofuro* bath in beautiful surroundings is a coveted luxury in Japan. This natural hot spring bath at the edge of the patio has a great ocean view and can also be used by the family on their way back from the ocean.

RING HOUSE

This small glass tower wrapped in alternating rings of wood and glass challenges the assumption that a vacation home in wooded hills should be a spread-out low building. The 102-square-meter Ring House was commissioned as a speculative venture by the developer of a planned community of 318 lots slightly removed from the center of the popular resort town of Karuizawa. Due to its location in a steep valley and the fact that the lot did not have the views of the mountains so sought after in Karuizawa, the developer decided to hire a young architectural firm TNA to see if they could turn this disadvantageous site into a saleable property. Architects Takei Makoto and Nabeshima Chie's first impression of the relatively large 1380 square meter site was of the beautiful groves of mature walnut, chestnut and larch trees, and the fact that the neighboring houses were not a major visual disturbance here due to the site's location in a valley.

The goal was to design a house from which views of the surrounding trees could be enjoyed from various heights. The architects chose a tall (11 meters high) and slender form (34 square meters) with the smallest possible footprint that displaced only three trees, and placed it on the northern section of the valley away from the three roads at the top of the site. The outstanding element of design here is the system of "rings"; glue-laminated panels that serve as structural beams, exterior walls as well as frames for the windows. All architectural components of the house, such as the floor slabs, stair landings, kitchen counter, ventilation hood and the wood-burning stove, were designed to fit within the dimensions of the rings so as not to be visible from outside. Only the staircase intersects the rings. The entrance hall and tatami-matted guest room are located on the half-basement entrance floor. The living, dining and kitchen areas are on the second floor, and the master bedroom and bathroom on the third floor. Every space has a great view of the woods, while the valley location provides a measure of privacy.

The number of colors and materials in the house has been kept to a minimum in order to emphasize the "rings." The exterior of these rings is finished with smoked *sugi* (Japanese cedar) wood while the interior of the rings, walls and ceilings have been painted with white acrylic emulsion paint. Wooden window frames that puncture the rings have been left unpainted as a design feature. The floors of the second and third levels are surfaced with birch wood. Except for the Hans Wegner's dining and lounge chairs, all furniture and furnishings have been designed by the architects as part of their design package, giving the house a sense of harmony.

Since Karuizawa is also becoming popular as a winter vacation area, the house has been winterized with an innovative heating system. The conventional electric floor heating provided in the living room and master bedroom has been supplemented by a hot water heating system that supplies heat through portable electric fan heaters that can be connected to wall outlets installed in each room. An electric hot air blower fan heats the bathroom. Fiber reinforced plastic has been used for waterproofing the roof. Special split ring joints were designed to bolt the reinforced concrete columns to exterior ring beams, which made it unnecessary to use additional earthquake resistant braces or panels.

The success of this project was confirmed when the lot with this house became one of the first properties to be sold in the development. It was purchased by a young product designer based solely upon seeing the photographs.

Previous spread The number of colors and materials in the house has been kept to a minimum in order to emphasize its "rings." The exterior of these rings is finished with smoked sugi (Japanese cedar) wood while the interior of the rings, walls and ceilings has been painted with white acrylic emulsion paint.

Right Wooden window frames that puncture the rings have been left unpainted as a design feature. The floors of the second and third levels are surfaced with birch wood.

Below The only element intersecting the rings is the staircase. The wooden bridge seen in the photograph leads directly to the second floor kitchen for carrying in groceries.

Above Wishbone chairs designed by Hans Wegner surround the beech wood dining table, which was custom designed by the architects. The lighting fixture in painted steel with a moveable arm was also custom designed for this project. Its exposed light bulb is a commercially available shatterproof product encased in plastic coating. The fireplace, kitchen counter and ventilation hood were also custom built to fit within the measurements of the "rings."

Above Except for the Hans Wegner's dining and lounge chairs, all furniture and furnishings have been designed by the architects as part of their design package, giving the house a sense of harmony.

Left and right The master bedroom and bathroom are located on the third floor. The bathroom is a split level up from the bedroom, divided by a low wall, with closets installed on the bedroom side and a sink installed on the bathroom side .The enameled bathtub is from German manufacturer Kaldewei. A luxurious *ofuro* soaking bath with a view of outdoors is every vacationer's dream in Japan, and this one has spectacular views all around.

TSURUMI
ATELIER +
RESIDENCE

This architect-owned atelier + residence is a celebration of the delicacy of Japanese design sensibilities. The surfaces of this 9-x-9-x-9-meter cubic concrete volume have been treated like a canvas on which rich textures and exquisite materials have been juxtaposed. These include *sugi* (cedar wood)–imprinted exposed concrete, furnishings made of *makore* (West African cherry) wood, tatami reed mats, shoji sliding screens, hammered terrazzo floors and rough polished "arai dashi" concrete pavement. The tactile and aesthetic qualities of these exquisite materials have been achieved through traditional Japanese craftsmanship and processes.

The 262–square-meter Tsurumi atelier + residence is built on a site where the architect has lived since he was two years old. As is customary for timber homes in Japan, the previous thirty-year-old house on this site was slated for rebuilding. This gave Nakagame Kiyonobu+Nakagame Kiyonobu Architect and Associates an opportunity to design a new home for his parents and himself, and include an atelier for this architecture practice in the basement. Nakagame had spent most of his school holidays as a child on construction sites with his father, a building contractor, and has a deep appreciation of the building craft. His understanding of the potential and beauty of various building materials is evident in this house. As an example, the architect wire brushed the sugi formwork himself to bring out its wooden grain and articulate the joints in between wooden planks to give it remarkable scale and texture. In another example, the terrazzo floor in the entrance hall was poured on site, and part of this floor was designed to have a rougher finish, which the architect achieved by diligently hammering the terrazzo by hand. He also laid Styrofoam insulations into 450-millimeter-thick concrete walls himself.

The site sits on top of a hill with a row of cherry blossom trees and a schoolyard on its northeast side. The architect has used his familiarity of the site to create an effective interface between the house and its surroundings. While the basement has been designed for privacy from the street, the second and third floors are completely open on the northeast sides to take maximum advantage of the cherry trees nearby. This concept of borrowed scenery is called *shakkei* and is a well-understood concept in Japanese garden and architecture design. The atelier is entered directly from the stairs leading from the street level to the sunken court. The entrance to the main house is accessed from a bridge over a lower court.

An elevator was installed for the convenience of the architect's aged father. The elevator shaft also acts as load bearing element, leaving other areas column-free. Timber flooring in the house as well as all the built-in furniture has been constructed using makore wood from a single large log that the architect's father had purchased in a lumberyard in Kiba thirty ago. The dining table, kitchen cabinets and the office desk are also custom-made from this wood. Teak wood has been used for the entrance, the bathroom and dressing rooms due to its durability in wet areas. Floor heating has been provided in the entire house. Louvers have been used to conceal all the air conditioning units.

This atelier + residence is also a good example of the subtle Japanese sensitivity of light and shadows that is so well described in Tanizachi Jun'ichiro's book *In Praise of Shadows*. The entrance to the atelier is down a staircase and through a sunken "light garden." Shafts of light that enter this area become design elements in the meditative quite space with textured concrete walls. Other areas of the house are either softly lit through shoji screens or frosted glass walls, or open to greenery.

Previous spread The open plan of the third floor provides a wonderful view of the treetops on the northeast and the cherry blossoms in spring.

Above This Japanese room is located off the entrance foyer. The sliding doors, which conceal a mini kitchen, are papered with persimmon-dyed *washi* paper while the smaller doors, which conceal a bedding closet, are finished with straw-embedded washi paper.

Right Arrangements of seasonal branches and flowers are set in this large pot discovered by the architect in a Chichibu antique shop. A large brass tray from Morocco hangs on the wall.

Left A collection of antique bowls sits in the modernized version of a tokonoma, an alcove for hanging screens and placing flower arrangements.

Right Built-in shelves in the living room hold books and collectibles.

Below left The brushed aluminum hooks that screw into the bolts formerly used to fasten the concrete formwork were designed by Architect Yokokawa Ken. These are now easily available due to the popularity of exposed concrete buildings in Japan. An antique *palang*, a bamboo woven container traditionally used to store and serve water and alcohol in Bhutan, hangs on one of these hooks.

Below middle The atelier does not feel like it is in the basement due to the sunshine and blooming rosemary bushes that border the sunken court facing the atelier. Continuation of the floor level and pattern on the inside and outside add to a feeling of spaciousness.

Below far right The traditional paper talisman to ward off fires came from a Shinto shrine that the architect has frequented since his childhood. It is affixed on the exposed concrete ledge designed to hold scale models of the architect's design projects in his atelier.

Below A tasteful mix of modern classics and rustic crafts are seen throughout the house. Here, a contemporary leather sofa and floor lamp are paired with an African stool and cushions covered with persimmon-dyed mulberry paper made by Richard Fleming and Yoko Haraguchi, who cultivate mulberry trees and other plants for their papers.

Bottom The carbonized ash–glazed ceramic piece in the sunken court facing the architect's workspace was originally one of the supports for shelves in a kiln in Shigaraki, an area well known for pottery.

Above The architect has used his familiarity of the site to create an effective interface between the house and its surroundings. The concept of borrowed scenery, or shakkei—a well-understood principle in Japanese design—is evident in this room. The cowhide-covered chaise lounge was designed by Le Corbusier in 1928.

Right The architect's understanding of the potential and beauty of various building materials is evident throughout this house. The architect wire brushed the sugi formwork himself to bring out its wooden grain and articulate the joints in between wooden planks to give it remarkable scale and texture.

K COURTYARD HOUSE

This project with a studio for the architect-owner and a house for his family is located in a 230-square-meter urban residential lot in Harara-cho area of Kagoshima. The project has been designed with special consideration for the owner's mother. She has been wheelchair bound since she was in an accident six years ago, and the owner wanted a house where she could enjoy the changing light, seasons, and other joys of nature from indoors. The result is a simple plan around a courtyard, with large windows and vistas designed from the vantage point of a person in a wheelchair.

The architect-owner of the house was a former staff member in Nakahara Yuji Architect Design Office of architect Nakahara Yuji. Instead of designing his own house, the owner decided to hire his former boss so that he could learn as much as possible from Nakahara through this project. The owner himself undertook site supervision of the 227-square-meter house. He concludes that the most important thing he learned from Nakahara is that architectural design at its best is a result of accumulation of the architect's experiences and his ability to interpret the client's sensitivity and needs. Such sensitivity on the part of Nakahara is probably the reason that this house feels very comfortable to the owner and his family.

The owner's studio is located at the front of the site and is accessed by an independent staircase. The house is located in the back across a courtyard with living areas placed on the second floor at a higher elevation than the studio. This allows those in the house to have a view of the pool above the entrance, the courtyard, the sky and even people walking in the front street across the wooded courtyard and studio. The master bedroom suite for the couple is on the third floor. The study at that level has been separated from the vaulted double-height stairwell of the living room by a punched metal screen. Ample storage space has been provided throughout the house in order to keep the living areas clutter-free. An elevator has been installed to enable the mother to reach the second floor and to use the bathroom at the lower level.

The courtyard is at the center of the plan. Although small, this courtyard has been landscaped with great skill and feels large due to the scrub brush and the grove of native deciduous trees that have been transplanted here from the mountains. The mother enjoys watching the plants change with the season, as well as birds and insects that visit this small garden-courtyard. The studio, the living room and the corridors have all been placed at different heights around this courtyard, and provide a different view of the landscaping. This relationship to the outdoors created for the mother has generated a sense of "discovery" for the whole family living in this house.

Natural materials have been used throughout the house for comfort, and in mostly exposed form in order to express their materiality. For example, the welding marks on the iron sheets for the fireplace (designed by architect Nakahara) were deliberately left exposed as part of the architect's philosophy of expressing the materials and processes used. Brazilian cherry wood is used for the exterior walls made of reinforced concrete. Cherry wood has also been used on the floors as it wears well with the floor heating provided throughout the house. The walls have been finished with plaster and painted white. Reinforced concrete walls not covered with cherry wood were cast in a formwork of wood designed to impart an interesting texture on the exposed concrete. The third floor has a steel structure, which is expressed in the H-shaped exposed column and iron plates. Together these materials create tranquil, well-proportioned and comfortable spaces in the house.

Previous spread The Brazilian cherry wood facing used for the exterior walls gives the exterior a strong red color as well as a sense of scale.

Left The red Utrecht armchair designed by Gerrit T. Rietveld in 1935 was sourced from Cassina.

Above The sloped courtyard between the studio and the house is covered with crushed stone.

Above The bathroom is a minimalist sanctuary. The floor, walls and the bathtub are lined with Shirakawa stone, a soft stone quarried in Fukushima Prefecture. A small pool located outside the glass wall of the bathtub is reflected in the mirror on its farther wall to create an illusion of an expansive water surface, and to provide daylight into the bathroom.

Right The galley kitchen has been located behind the living room bookshelf.

Below A small study is built next to the master bedroom on the third floor.

Far right Visual continuity across rooms and floors gives this house a spacious feeling.

Opposite page and top left The staircase is made of iron and has wooden treads. The entire wall behind the staircase has been made into bookshelves to accommodate the large collection of books owned by the family. Furniture and fixtures such as this bookshelf have been effectively used as space dividers without blocking off the flow of space in the house.

Bottom left and above The long tunnel-like entrance hall leading to the residence has a trough shaped glass ceiling filled with crushed stone and water. Natural light shining through the spaces between the stones creates a dynamic light and shadow effect on the bare walls and floor.

Top Skillful landscaping makes this small lot seem like a natural wooded area, with various indigenous trees transplanted here from the mountains.

IZUMIYA

Water and stone are the two essential elements of Izumiya, a remarkable house constructed in 1972. This twentieth-century house has been included in this book for its response to two timeless issues in Japanese design: the quests to express the innate beauty of natural materials and to bring the interior and exterior closer together. These goals have been achieved in this house by using traditional materials such as stones, shoji screens, timber floors and tatami mats in a radically different way than in traditional Japanese architecture.

Izumiya is the product of a symbiotic relationship between the late architect Yamamoto Tadashi, the owner Izumi Masatoshi, and the influence of the renowned sculptor Isamu Noguchi, with whom both of them had worked closely. The client is from a family of stonemasons in Mure, an area famous for production and processing of fine granite known as *aji-ishi*. However, his family got its name from another town located south of Osaka, made famous during the sixteenth century when stonemasons from China and Korea taught masonry techniques to Japanese builders in Izumi Town. Many of these builders later moved on to live in the town of Mure in Shikoku Island, but carried the name Izumi with them.

The use of stone in Izumiya is a reflection of Izumi Masatoshi's philosophy. He founded Stone Atelier in 1964 to explore better ways of expressing the innate beauty of stones. In keeping with eastern thought where the observer and the observed are part of the same whole, Izumi feels a strong identification with stones he works with, and considers distorting them from their inherent characteristics an undesirable practice. He seeks to create forms where the soul of each stone is expressed in as natural a way as possible, and believes that one must handle a stone created by natural forces over thousands of years with great humility.

The ground floor of this 267-square-meter house is composed of massive stone masonry walls, a light steel space frame and roof, and an occasional reed ceiling. A continuous strip window below the ceiling level adds to the impression of airiness of the roof that contrasts with the heavy stonewalls below. Innovative use of stones of various shapes and colors in the walls, floors and artifacts has produced a powerful experience. The entire glass wall of the living room can be slid aside to open the room to the porch and the garden. A small second floor area has two tatami-matted bedrooms and a wooden truss, lending it a more traditional than the first floor.

The central feature of the living room is a column constructed from two pieces of solid granite. Since stone looks best when it is wet, this column, the rough ashlar stone floor, stone alcoves, and other stone objects of this room are watered every day. As this is common practice in Japanese gardens, the effect of this in Izumiya is the blurring of the distinction between inside and outside. Indoor plants that grow out of the stone crevices further reinforce that concept.

To this day the stonemason Izumi continues to chisel, hammer and polish natural stones that he selects from the family's stock of stone brought from nearby mountain quarries. He is committed to maintaining the history and traditions of his birthplace, the stonemason's town of Mure. He believes that Isamu Noguchi was also deeply influenced by the spirit of this town. Architect Yamamoto who traveled with Noguchi to India and then America to visit Georgia O'Keefe, believes that the work of Noguchi and Izumi springs from their global outlook as well as their local roots.

Previous spread The six tatami-mat tearoom embodies the timeless beauty of stone and the aesthetic of *wabi-sabi* (understated beauty that is acquired with age). The steel space frame ceiling is covered with *yoshizu* reed screens.

Left The new residence wing has been built next to Izumiya. The *tsubo-niwa* (small enclosed garden) seen here is located between the stonewall of Izumiya and glass wall of the entrance hall. The stone washbasin is called *tsukubai* and literally translates as "to crouch, sit, bow," refering to the humble posture that visitors are expected to be in while they cleanse and purify themselves with water before entering a Zen temple or teahouse.

Above The mud-walled building is a reclaimed sake brewery that Izumi reconstructed on the vast grounds that also house the Isamu Noguchi Garden Museum. Originally built for Noguchi's studio as a birthday present shortly before his death, it is now shared by offices for both Izumi's practice and the Isamu Noguchi foundation.

Above An old earthenware octopus trap arranged with a single camellia bloom sits in the tokonoma alcove. The floor of the tokonoma is constructed from a single slab of polished aji-ishi measuring 66 centimeters by 2.7 meters.

Above left Located behind the entrance foyer, a moss-covered courtyard leads to the tearoom seen in the background.

Left The dining room is also made of stone masonry walls. Noguchi's paper lanterns hang above the rustic table of zelcova wood called *keyaki* in Japanese. The door behind leads to the kitchen.

Above The attic of the old sake brewery serves as a guest room and a spectacular gallery for Isamu Nogushi's renowned light sculpture series known as *Akari*, which means "light" in Japanese.

Left The column in the living room is constructed from two pieces of solid granite. The top of the column is capped with a piece of wood that was carved out to make the large hole in "Black Sun," a sculpture created by Isamu Noguchi in 1969 that is now in the Seattle Art Museum. Noguchi's tool marks have been left intact as a testament to the stone's history.

Above right The timber staircase is nestled in the stone structure in a manner that articulates the beauty of both materials. A sink carved out of single slab of aji-ishi has been installed in front of the bathroom.

Above far right and right "31N," from one of Noguchi's paper light sculpture series entitled Akari hangs in the corner of the entrance foyer.

NOBORIGAMA HOUSE

Yokohama was one of the earliest ports opened to foreign trade during the Meiji Period, and its people take pride in their daring spirit. This spirit came in useful in the design and building of this house. The owner had bought this plot of land just after looking at a promotional rendering of a house in an advertisement. However, he later found out that the site was at a 35-degree incline and nearly impossible to build on. Several architects and contractors had actually refused to take on the design of the house before Tanijiri Makoto of Suppose Design and Nawa Kanji+Nawakenjim accepted the commission.

Noborigama, the name of this 138-square-meter house, actually comes from the climbing kilns used in traditional pottery making in Japan. These kilns are located on hills and take advantage of natural breezes to set up convection currents of rising hot air for firing pots. The architect took this inspiration to design a remarkable house for a couple with two grown children on this very difficult site.

Since 80 percent of the site is steep, concrete retaining walls had to be built into the hill side, and piles driven into the level part of the site. Steel frame construction has been used for the superstructure.

The architect and the client both wanted to build a house that would capitalize on the spectacular view from this site of the northeast of Bay Bridge in Yokohama. Every room in the house has been designed to make the most of this view. Another design goal was to make maximum possible use of the site characteristics to reduce dependence on mechanical heating, cooling and ventilation. Although the slope of the site made it hard to build upon, it actually aids in the natural passive cooling and heating of this house. In summer the breeze from the ocean passes around and under the house keeping it cool, while the windows have been designed for passive solar heating during winter. Under-floor heating has been provided in each room.

The aesthetics system of the house sets out to make a virtue of a difficult building situation. While the walls on ether end of the house have been finished in white paint, the floors as well as ceilings have been made of wood. This system has been consistently followed on all the levels, thus giving the entire house a sense of unity. The floors have been made of Brazilian hard cherry finished with oil, while the ceilings are made of *karin* wood. A staircase that climbs all the way up from the bottom to the top of the house forms an important visual axis, and has been treated as such. The remarkable clarity of the plan in this house has resulted in architecture that is user friendly and also dramatic at the same time.

Previous page The aesthetics system of the house sets out to make a virtue of a very steep building site. While the walls on ether end of the house have been finished in white paint, the floors as well as ceilings have been made of wood.

Right Simplicity of furniture and architecture details focuses the eyes on the spectacular view seen through full-height mullion-less glazing.

Above left A spectacular night view of Bay Bridge can be enjoyed from the dining room. The dining table seen in the foreground is designed by the renowned architect Le Corbusier. The Saffron dining chairs are from Ixc.

Far left Built-in furniture such as the kitchen counter and the ceiling have been made of karin wood. Patricia Urquiola designed the "Last Minute" kitchen chairs that have been manufactured by Cassina.

Left The bathroom with a sloped ceiling is situated behind the dining and kitchen areas.

Top left Effective use of lighting built into the vanity fixtures adds drama to the bathroom finished in karin wood and slate tiles. All sanitary fixtures are from German manufacturer Hans Grohe.

Top right A simple flower arrangement sits in a corner of the built-in shelf and cupboards designed to hold CDs.

Above The modular Ile sofa designed by Piero Lissoni provides for ample and flexible seating for guest interaction and TV viewing. The long ottoman can be connected to any part of the sofa to suit various needs. The floor lamp is from Cassina. A recently developed popular product, tatami-mat tiles allow homeowners to make Japanese seating areas wherever they please.

Above A whimsical table lamp called Hana designed by Marei sits on the built-in furniture, much like a flower arrangement.

Above right and far right The staircase climbing all the way up from the bottom to the top of the house forms an important visual axis.

Right The master bedroom with a stylish woven leather bed is located on the uppermost level of the four-storied house. Every room in this house has been designed to make the most of the Bay Bridge view.

JOGASAKI KAIGAN HOUSE

Can a house really help build a vacation into your everyday life? That is what a family from Tokyo aimed to do in this weekend house that is also expected to become the parents' permanent home after retirement. Due to this dual program requirement, the location for this house had to be not only beautiful, but also have easy access to necessary shopping and conveniences. These requirements were met in a subdivision in Ito City on the Pacific Coast in Shizuoka Prefecture, with beautiful views of Suruga Bay in the south and Mount Omuro in the north. The 855-square-meter site is located along a cherry tree–lined road that leads to the Jogasaki coast. Since the site is within a third category scenic national park area, land and development laws restrict the ground coverage of each lot and require that each property be designed to preserve the flora and fauna of this special location. The result is a development where nature can still be enjoyed in spite of the many houses that have been built there.

The clients wanted the exterior as well as interior of the house to convey a sense of excitement about getting away from the daily work routine. Architect Ishii Hideki+Ishii Hideki Architect Atelier chose to symbolize this concept via a large sculpturesque roof that mimics the contours of the site so that wind flows and the natural topography of the site was not disturbed. The site originally had two shallow hills on its east and west sides that were carefully studied, and the roof designed accordingly. However, upon further examination, the eastern hill was found to be unstable and had to be flattened and replaced by the two-storied bedroom block.

This 129-square-meter house was designed for a family of five, including a couple, two daughters and one pet dog. The architectural program has been articulated into three distinct blocks with the central living space flowing between and around them. The three blocks hold the bedrooms, the guest room and the garage respectively, and have been located at the three corners under the large roof. The parking block has been located on the north where the row of cherry blossom trees leads to the entrance. The two-storied bedroom block is on the eastern corner where the small hill had been flattened, and the guest block is on the west. The double-height living area flows in between these blocks and opens out toward the tree-filled open spaces around the house allowing the breeze, views of sky and changing light to flow through the house. The flow of these natural elements was considered an absolute requirement in this space, while the remaining blocks may need to respond to the clients' changing needs over a period of time.

The entire pentagonal plan of the house is turned at a 45-degree angle to the square site in order to avoid having windows face the neighbors directly. Besides providing privacy, this also allowed the open spaces to be used more effectively than would have been possible if the house had been located parallel to the site edges. The architect believes that in addition to addressing the program with clarity and simplicity, truly successful architecture must also be flexible and inspiring so as to transcend the mundane daily activities of a family and make living in the house a special experience.

Previous spread The exterior walls are finished with smoked Japanese cedar with a special coating. Wood and aluminum frames have been used for the windows due to the site's proximity to the ocean.

Left Built at an angle, the kitchen counter adds geometric interest to the large living and dining room.

Above The double-height living area flows between the two bedroom blocks and opens out toward the tree-filled open spaces around the house.

Near right A contemporary "bonsai" sits in the modernized white ash tokonoma alcove.

Far right The dramatic play of light and shadow is further accentuated by the clever use of dark- and light-colored wood. The platform stairs lead to the hallway connecting to the two-storied bedroom block on the east corner of the house.

Above left The modern Japanese room is fitted with square borderless *rikyu* tatami mats, a popular choice among contemporary architects.

Above right The ceiling lamp "33N" from the Akari Light Sculpture series designed by Isamu Noguchi is a dramatic presence in the cathedral ceiling of the living room. The dining table has been custom designed in white ash by the architect. Its 3-meter-long span is made of 60-millimeter-thick timber and has been supported by a framework within the table so that no supporting beam was required. The Baguette dining chairs are designed by Igarashi Hisae and manufactured by Hida Sangyo.

Right The architect has filled a galvanized steel trough outside the window with white pebbles to provide an interesting visual border to the traditional rock garden. This modernized *tsubo-niwa* (the small enclosed garden) offsets the dark tone of the smoked Japanese cedar well.

Middle right In winter, the *engawa* separates the inside and outside of the house, while in summer it fuses them.

Far right The use of shoji screens that can be slid away to open the entire living/dining room wall also dramatically transforms the ambience of the room.

Above Many rocks were excavated from the site during the construction of this house, creating the perfect opportunity to create a rock garden. The owner's relative, a gardener residing nearby, designed the garden.

Top right A wood-burning stove lends a warm ambiance to the living room. Unlike the fussy detailing of commercially available fireplaces, the glass cover of this one has been carefully designed by the architect to be flush with its structure, giving it a neat appearance so well appreciated in Japanese design.

Right The living and dining area has the minimum amount of furniture as the owners enjoy sitting on the floor.

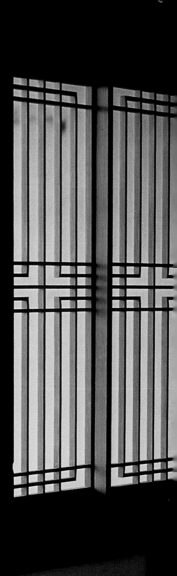

SHEET METAL TEAHOUSE

This addition to a *minka* farmhouse and the teahouse are an elegant solution to the universal challenge of combining modernity and comfort with traditional vernacular architecture.

The owner's father had built this minka in the outskirts of Osaka eighty years ago. While it was one of several such houses in this area at that time, it is remarkable today that it has survived the real estate speculation and rebuilding all around it. However, with the exception of the structural framework and the front exterior, all other parts of it have been drastically changed or remodeled over the years. Architect Kimura Hiroaki of Ks Architects sought to restore it to its original condition relying on the memory of the owner's father and other surviving minka houses.

The style of the original building combines elements of minka farmhouses as well as elegant *sukiya*-style homes. This mixture is unusual in other parts of Japan but common in this area. It was probably developed because landowners here required the practicality of farmhouses for storage and work tools, but aspired to own sukiya homes like their counterparts in the city. During the restoration work, all previous additions and alterations that were not in the spirit of the original building were stripped, and a new addition that neither competes with nor compromises the dignity of the old farmhouse was added.

This 176-square-meter home for a family of four and their pet dog now consists of the old minka, the new addition and the teahouse in the garden. The architect has used steel plates and glass block as the predominant building materials for the new construction. His preference for using steel plate structures goes back fifteen years, inspired by the curved metal forms of trains and ships. Although his earlier experiments with corrugated galvanized metal buildings were less than satisfactory, he soon realized the structural as well as aesthetic potential of 9-millimeter-thick steel sheets for smaller projects such as residences and churches. It was also a good coincidence that 9-millimeter steel was easy to get roll-pressed to exact shapes and dimensions.

While interior partitions of the addition have been made of 9-millimeter steel sheets, this material has been combined with insulation and interior finishes to make up 100-millimeter-thick exterior walls. The impact of steel sheets is well articulated in the 8.5-meter-long walls of the corridor that separates the old and new construction. Steel angle ribs have been used here instead of traditional columns and are placed 960 millimeters apart, in the same rhythm as the columns of the old minka. This method of construction is similar to that used for constructing living quarters of boats. While the architect usually specifies paint on steel surfaces, he chose to leave them unfinished in this project as they worked well with the rustic, un-hewn timbers of the farmhouse.

In contrast to the addition to the minka, the free form of the metal teahouse makes it a sculptural presence in the garden. The semi-open exterior, the walls and roof are one continuous steel surface designed in response to the traditional garden that the owner's father had tended for many years. It is also part of the architect's long-term desire to create monocoque skin structures that are not dependent upon columns and beams. The plan of the teahouse, which is quite different from the other symmetrical buildings designed by him, is asymmetical in order to accommodate the pine tree that stands in front of it. The structure was assembled in a factory, divided into two parts, transported to the site, and lowered into the garden by a crane. Its parts were then reconnected, fittings inserted, and interior furnishings—the alcove and two tatami mats—were added. Its size was influenced by the size of vehicles that transported it, while its form lends it structural strength.

The exterior and interior of the teahouse have been given different aesthetic expressions. While the interior has traditional accoutrements such as a tokonoma alcove and tatami mats, the exterior is finished with a smooth industrial heat-resistant paint similar to that used for automobiles. The sliding doors are made of MDF. However, these modern materials and construction techniques come together to create a meditative quality similar to that found in traditional teahouses.

Previous spread and above Located in a mature traditional Japanese garden, the new teahouse is seen here from the old farmhouse. This precast monocoque structure was lifted by cranes into this garden so as to cause it minimum possible disturbance.

Left Traces of the fabrication process and welding have been left in the tokonoma and interior of this ultramodern teahouse. Such devices are meant to show the passage of time, and are typically included in traditional Japanese teahouses.

Above The semi-open form of the teahouse allows a dialogue between the inside and outside of this garden structure.

Below (left to right) A new staircase was built up to the attic of the old minka house. Shoe closets have been fitted in the space below in the style of the traditional *kaidan dansu*. The latticed entrance door casts striking vertical shadows in the entrance foyer. Traditional accouterments at the entrance to the teahouse are seen here, including the stone washbasin called *tsukubai* for visitors to cleanse and purify themselves before entering and a *machiai* bench for visitors to wait until invited into the teahouse.

Right A lower level wing made up of a passage with a skylight, the kitchen and dining area were added as connectors between the old and the new parts, symbolizing the bridging of traditional and a modern lifestyles. The new addition houses the bedrooms and bathroom.

Opposite page Inspired by the curved metal forms of trains and ships, the opening in the steel wall leading to the bathroom also has curved corners. A *kamidana*, a miniature Shinto shrine with an offering of rice, flowers and water, is seen above the skylight louvers. Such shrines are common in many traditional homes.

Above An old newspaper from 1929 was found stuck to one of the walls. This has been covered with glass to preserve the memory of the minka's past. A *gohei* (Shinto Staff) was also discovered in the attic during restoration work, a silent witness to the fact that the ridgepole of the old minka had been raised on November 1925.

Left and below In spite of the use of ultramodern materials, the teahouse has the quality of stillness found in traditional teahouses.

OCEAN VILLA

Previous spread The straightforward box shape of the second floor has been articulated with a frame of galvanized steel, which surrounds a composition of white plaster and light-brown smoked pinewood elements. These materials were selected in response to the harsh ocean-side environment.

Above and right All the chairs in the Ocean Villa are from Ritzwell, the house owner's company. The exceptions are the PP 19 armchairs (1951) in the living room from Hans Wegner, a furniture designer whom the owner is very fond of. Appreciation of good furniture runs in the family, as the oldest son of the owner is also currently studying furniture design.

Left The living, dining and kitchen on the second floor open out to a spacious deck facing the ocean.

The Ocean Villa is located about a thirty-minute drive on the highway from the center of Fukuoka City. Although within the city limits, the site is a part of a second category national park system, which restricts lot coverage to only twenty percent in order to preserve the many trees and shrubs here. This area is also close to Yobuko of Saga Prefecture, a place known for fresh squid sashimi. The scenic views and easy accessibility of this development from the surrounding fishing areas makes it a popular choice for retirement homes.

Architect Imoto Shigemi+Imoto Architects worked with the owner right from the site selection process. The owner had known the architect previously in connection with his furniture business, but decided to entrust the design of his house to him after visiting another house designed by this architect in the same development. The goal for this house was to create a place where the family could gather on weekends with a soothing view of the ocean, and where the owners could live after the husband retires from his furniture business in Fukuoka.

The 2500-square-meter site sits on a slope, with the flat buildable area several meters below the approach road. Because the foliage from the neighboring lot obstructs the view of the ocean at that level, the architect decided to put the living and dining areas on the second floor, which offers wide-open views. The foundation and first floor level have been constructed of reinforced concrete, while steel frame construction has been used for the much larger second floor. The concrete foundation has also been designed to enclose a studio. Although not part of the original program, this space was created to maximize the usable space.

The kitchen and living and dining rooms on the second floor open out to a spacious deck facing the ocean and a small balcony on the south side. The very small lower two floors, and the large living area on the second floor with its cantilevered deck, give this house an appearance of a floating box pointed toward the sea. The strong colors of the second floor exteriors and the recessive color of the concrete lower floors reinforce this image when seen from the approach road.

This 195-square-meter house has a few luxurious details that make the experience of living here special. The bathroom has been located on the second floor along with the living areas to enable enjoyment of the great ocean view. Natural light and the feeling of openness in the bathroom make soaking in the *ofuro* tub truly relaxing. While toilets are increasingly being attached to bedrooms in modern Japanese homes, the ofuro, like a Swedish sauna, is a more communal experience, and is often located where the entire family can comfortably use it. The entire glass wall on the ocean side, as well as the large windows on the south of the living area, can be opened for cross-ventilation during the summer, while floor heating and a wood stove keep the house usable in winter.

In each of the houses Imoto designs, he likes to blur the boundaries between the outside and inside of the house. The exposed concrete wall and the 300-millimeter-thick unpolished marble flooring connect the approach to the entry hall in a manner that does just that. This wall was cast in a formwork carefully made of brushed red cedar timber, so it has the scale and pattern unique to wood. Artistically placed horizontal voids on this wall add to the aesthetic experience of entering this special house.

Far left From the bathroom area in the foreground, the entrance hall in the middle, and the living room at the far end, space flows together to create a feeling of openness in the house.

Left The living room gets flooded with sunlight, keeping it comfortable during winter.

Right The use of knotted pine flooring and light-colored wood/woven leather furniture with white upholstery complement the casual ocean lifestyle.

Below The unclear borders between inside and outside increase the feeling of expansiveness of the house. Café-style glass doors facing the spacious ocean-side deck slide fully open to bring in the ocean breeze.

Opposite page The neutral color used on the entrance hall walls sets off the sun-filled living and dining area.

Above While most of the site surrounding the house was left in its original condition, an arbor for barbeques and relaxation has been built on the lower slope of the land. A few other landscaping elements in keeping with the natural harmony of the site are also planned for the future.

Above left Artistically placed horizontal voids in the exposed concrete wall leading to the entrance add to the aesthetic experience of entering this special house.

Left The exposed concrete wall was cast in a formwork carefully made of brushed red cedar timber, so it has the scale and pattern unique to wood.

WHOLE EARTH PROJECT

Often called the Greenwich Village of Tokyo, Shimokitazawa is a unique and charming neighborhood with lively narrow streets and cafés filled with a diverse mix of people. Large buildings jostle with small wooden homes here in a typical Tokyo fashion. Part of its vibrancy comes from the healthy mix of residential and small business properties, and the community that loves living there. While parts of this neighborhood are slated for redevelopment in the near future, local citizens' organizations are demanding that its human scale and texture be maintained in some way, a movement rare in a city where people seldom question government decisions. Given this background, it is not surprising that the owner of this 113-square-meter house—named Whole Earth Project—made the property's relationship with its neighborhood and the world one of the criteria for its design. While the interface of this house to the neighborhood may be considered too forbidding by some, the goal is certainly noteworthy.

Architect Niizeki Kenichiro+Niizeki Studio shared the owner's concern for designing the house to not just to express individuality, but as a timeless and neutral unit of the cityscape. He sought to create its street interface with the objective of not necessarily blending in with the neighborhood, but with the idea that it could help make the street and neighborhood a better place. The result is a street front composed of two windowless rectangular monolithic forms, absolute in their neutrality and solidity. The architect arrived at these by searching for a form that would not look like an object that just dropped on to the site, but something that grew out if it and belongs there.

This house has been designed to accommodate the owner's workplace, a mix that is quite common in Shimokitazawa. The client asked that the separation between the inside and outside of the house, as well as between its workplace and residential functions, balance the requirements of privacy and openness. This was a challenge on this small site in a bustling district filled with densely packed shops and houses. This request was met by designing the entrance recessed between the two monolithic forms of exposed concrete blocks. The entrance is through a staircase that leads to the second floor terrace. From here one has the option of going into the office area on one side or the residential area on the other. Both these segments of the house have their own staircases to descend to the first floor, which cannot be accessed from the street. Large openings have been designed in the areas opening on to the terrace on the first floor as well as to the garden on the ground floor.

The structure system for the house consists of a relatively new construction method using reinforced masonry blocks of 200 × 200 × 400 millimeters. In this system, the core of the concrete blocks is filled with reinforced concrete, making them three or four times stronger than usual concrete block walls. These color-tinted blocks have been exposed on the exterior as well as the interior of the house. Environmental considerations encouraged the architect to have these cast in molds used for ordinary concrete blocks, thus reducing the wastage of wood in formwork as well as additional construction noise. No scaffolding was needed for the house since it was built from the inside out, thus enabling construction right up to the property line even within this crowded area. The relatively quite and waste-free construction process, where blocks were slowly laid by hand, was a unique spectacle to watch in a city where most buildings take shape hidden from the street view behind a cover of construction shroud and accompanied by loud mechanical noises.

Previous spread The lightness of the white mesh furniture Me´n designed by Jean-Marie Massaud contrasts with the dark solidity of the concrete block walls.

Above The object in the upstairs courtyard designed by Patrick Chia named "Cousin of objects with an existential crisis, I a stool too" is made from FRP and produced by Time & Style.

Opposite top The exterior staircase leads up to the second floor terrace where one has the option of going into the office area on one side, or the residential area on the other.

Opposite bottom (left to right) The street entrance is recessed in-between the two monolithic forms of exposed concrete blocks. A small Japanese room is located on the second floor of a third monolithic block. Two skylights pour light into the double-height office area and its partial mezzanine. This light is all the more dramatic because of the dark and heavy interior lit only by one small window and borrowed light from the entrance foyer.

Left A pair of Zepher chairs in sycamore wood from Time & Style sit in the entrance foyer paved with *fukaiwa*, a soft stone quarried in Tochigi Prefecture. A pivot door swings open to the *tsubo niwa* (a small enclosed garden).

Above The walk-in closet faces the enclosed garden. A woven bamboo Hizuki floor lamp designed by Marei casts a warm glow.

Above left All of the exterior spaces are paved with gravel to blend with the dark concrete block walls.

Right An internal staircase leads from the ground floor office to the meeting room located directly above. Being public areas, there is no need for shoe removal. The office flooring is *keisoudo*, a packed earth floor made of diatomite—a soft, chalklike sedimentary stone that crumbles into a fine white powder. The floor finish in the upstairs meeting room is in *ipe*, a Brazilian hardwood. A vintage Eames chair sits at the meeting table above.

HOUSE IN THE FOREST

This tiny house in its forest surroundings designed by architect Hasegawa Go of Hasegawa Go & Associates appears as if it may have come out of a fairy tale. Its barnlike dark form, steep ridged roof and punched windows are caricature-like in their simplicity. If you thought one has to choose between a pitched roofed cottage and a place to enjoy the forest from the roof top, the design of this house challenges that expectation with a playful balcony that juts out from the slope of its pitched roof. Located in a forest in Karuizawa on a site between a boardwalk on the north side and a small stream on its south, the design of this house seeks to bring the changing delights and seasons of the forest inside every room from various directions.

An innovative feature of this 90-square-meter house is a secondary gable ceiling built just a few feet below the roof. The space between the roof and the ceiling becomes flooded with daylight from the skylights during the day. The translucent surface of the ceiling acts like a reflex board of a camera, bringing the special effects of changing light and swaying tree shadows into each room. This translucent ceiling is made up of handmade Japanese *washi* paper applied to clear acrylic panels hung on a wooden framework in the bedroom. In the living room, maple veneer adhered to clear acrylic has been used for this purpose. Depending upon the time of the day, one or the other part of this ceiling lights up like a lantern as the sunlight streams in. Large as well as small rooms in the house have their own gabled ceiling. Since such ceilings present a much larger surface to the interior than flat ceilings, their effect on the perception of a room has been well understood and exploited by the young architect for this house. This double roof also has the added benefit of helping insulate interior spaces in the cold winters of Karuizawa.

The space between the pitched ceilings of the entrance hall and guest room has resulted in an unusual loft with a sloping surface for its floor. Climbing up the staircase from the entrance lobby to the balcony through this playfully meditative space is a special experience that culminates as one reaches the balcony surrounded by the trees, breeze and the sound of the rushing brook nearby.

Each room also has its own distinct and contrasting interior design features, which heightens the awareness of each space as one moves through the house.

Previous page and above Located in a dense forest, this house gets its striking dark silhouette from the 0.4-millimeter-thick formed galvanized steel plates on the roof as well as the walls.

Near left The living room, seen here through a bedroom door, is accessed from the entrance as well as the bedrooms, wasting no space on corridors in this small house.

Far left This translucent ceiling is made up of handmade Japanese washi paper applied to clear acrylic panels.

Right A person working in the kitchen has visual access to the living room as well as the light-filled geometry of the space between the living room ceiling and the roof. Such visual devices make this house appear much larger than it actually is.

Above Each room has its own distinct interior design characteristics. The wood tones in the living room contrast with the dark finishes in the guest room and the white walls of the bedroom.

Left and below The space between the pitched ceilings of the entrance hall and guest room has resulted in an unusual loft with a sloping surface for its floor.

Below right A surprisingly playful balcony juts out from the slope of the pitched roof.

Next page All floor and wall surfaces have been finished with moisture retardant FRP coating. Floor hearing has been provided in all rooms since Karuizawa has very cold winters. The living room floor is made of maple wood. The walls are finished with oil-stained plywood, while the ceiling is made of maple veneer on clear acrylic hung on wooden framework.

This two-storied house on a large site in Yokohama City, Kanagawa Prefecture accommodates three separate units for an extended family. The father and the families of his two sons wanted to have a house with common areas, as well as their own private spaces where they could continue to enjoy the independent lifestyles they had in city apartments prior to moving here. This solution is a good alternative to the trend of increasingly smaller individual family lots in Japan, and also enables the children to enjoy staying close to aging parents and grandparents. The architects Yagi Masashi and Konomi of Yagi Architectural Design worked on the overall concept of the house in consultation with the whole family to create a design well suited to the site topography and surroundings. The clients were presented with various alternate blocking arrangements untill they were pleased with the location and concept of the three units within the outer shell. After that the architects worked with the three families separately to design three distinct units to suit their tastes, right down to the color and material selection. The result is three units that express the personality of the three families, and yet fit harmoniously into the overall design.

This 498-square-meter house is situated on a steep southern slope in the hilly part of Yokohama city. Since mid-rise condominiums stand just across the road to the north of the site, privacy from that direction was an important consideration. This was addressed very early in the design process during a site visit, when the architects decided to screen off that side with a large earthen wall facade with just a few small openings in it. This wall is made of *shirasu soton*, a traditional Japanese material with volcanic ash known for its durability in high humidity areas. It became an important feature of the house plan and facade that stretches from east to west at the northern end of the site at the approach road. All living areas of the house open onto the large common green area on the south and also enjoy the sunlight from that direction. The eastern part of the house hugs the angular corner of the site to further enclose the shared green open space. The roof at this end has been extended to also serve as an entrance porch and garage. This bold projection has been balanced with a low wall on the western side of the earthen wall to form the entrance for the younger son's family.

The double-storied eastern wing houses the eldest son, his wife and their child. It includes a large open-plan kitchen and dining area. The middle section of the second floor is meant for the father, while the two-storied western wing is for the second son, his wife and their two children. The entrance for the father and the older son's family is on the eastern corner of the second floor, which, due to the slope of the road, is at street level. The entrance for the younger son's family in the western wing is located on the first floor at the bottom of a flight of steps.

A hybrid structural system has been used for the house, with reinforced concrete deployed for the first floor and a wooden structure for the second floor. Concrete boundary walls between each unit ensure sound privacy. This structural system has been visually expressed by the exposed concrete ceilings at the first floor level and reed-covered ceilings with rafters all through the second floor.

Natural materials have been used in the house as far as possible. Solid wood flooring has been used throughout, of the type selected by each client. While the father selected cypress flooring for his unit, the older son's family preferred teakwood, and chestnut wood was the choice of the younger son's family. The father's unit has a traditional Japanese atmosphere due to the wooden finishes and shoji screens used there. All interior walls are plastered and painted white, except for the rear face of the earthen wall at the street facade, which is exposed. Traditional diatom plaster with trowel finish has been used for the kitchen walls to control dampness and smell. Since diatom walls absorb and trap formaldehyde, a major cause of sick-building syndrome, this traditional material is once again becoming popular in Japan.

An aqua layer regenerative floor heating system has been used throughout the house. This system uses thermal water storage located between the floor joists in the father's unit and younger son's unit and is heated during the night when the power charges are low. The floor heating system in slightly different in the older son's unit, in that the concrete floor slab is used for thermal storage instead of water.

Right and left The father's unit has a comfortable traditional Japanese atmosphere due to the wooden finishes, shoji screens and the reed-covered ceilings, reminiscent of the thatched roofs of old farmhouses, used here. An AJ Royal pendant light designed by Arne Jacobsen for Loius Poulsen hangs above the dining table.

Below right A skylight in the father's unit makes acts as a wall washer to highlight the textured plaster wall.

Below left The apartment for the younger son's family has its own distinct character.

Above The glass wall of this open kitchen and dining area slides open to the large garden on the south.

Above near left The eldest son's wife, who is a cooking teacher, chose to have a tatami-matted study for cozy comfort. Beneath the long built-in desk, the floor has a sunken pit for her legs to drop into.

Above far left A play of light and shadow is provided throughout the day from the long and narrow skylight located above the entrance.

Left The southern facade, seen here, has a warm wood finish. This face opens toward the garden shared by all the members of the family.

Right The *shirasu soton* type earthen wall facade on the street side is surfaced with textured volcanic ash plaster.

YATSUGATAKE HOUSE

Located 1,500 meters above sea level at the foot of Mount Yastugatake in Minamimaki (Nagano Prefecture), this house is surrounded by rich woodland of larch and wild pear trees and a generous cropping of rare native chigo lilies (*disprum smilacinum*). It enjoys spectacular views in all directions and is far removed from other houses, with only the sound of wind and birds to disturb its quiet, a rare luxury in Japan. Architect Horibe Yasushi+Horibe Yasushi Architect & Associates has striven to distill the majesty of this landscape into a timeless geometric form.

This 152-square-meter house has been designed with the smallest possible footprint to minimize its impact on the site. Horibe started the design with a cruciform shape, with lean-to volumes at each corner so that the entire plan forms a perfect square. This simple design belies the effort needed to preserve the simplicity of an architect's early sketch without compromising the spatial and technical requirements of a house.

Conventional wooden construction methods have been deployed in this house designed for year-round use. Since winter temperatures in Yastugatake area average minus 10 degrees Celsius, protection from snow and frost is an important design consideration. Commercially available weather resistant double-glazed windows were selected for this reason, and glazing kept to a minimum in the bedrooms. The stairwell has been designed to aid in lighting, ventilation and temperature control. The bath and kitchen areas have been placed on the second floor directly above the machine room to facilitate plumbing. Heating ducts, water supply pipes and drainage pipes are all exposed in the machine room, allowing for easy maintenance. The machine room also doubles as a laundry drying area in winter.

The entrance porch of this house is referred to as *doma*, so named after the packed earth entrance areas common in traditional Japanese farmhouses. This area was used for cooking, crafts and tethering farm animals in the past. The doma here is finished with rough-hewn Shirakawa stone, a soft stone quarried in Fukushima Prefecture.

The spaces in the house have been arranged on five split-levels in the form of a spiral, with each lean-to at a different height. Careful consideration has been given to the pace, mood, light and texture suitable for the client's various activities. Interior walls have been plaster finished, while the floors and the ceilings are finished with Sawara cypress wood. Built-in furniture has been designed to help preserve the integrity of the architecture and reduce the clutter of conventional furniture.

Previous spread The architect Horibe is known for skilled woodwork details. He compares architecture to literal text and refers to architectural materials as the "words or phrases" and details as the "grammar" that governs them.

Left Of note are the custom-built double-paned sliding glass doors and the finely grooved wood railings in this living room area.

Above Horibe believes that a house plan is the key to good architecture, and should be thoroughly resolved to a point where the elevations, sections and details can logically flow from it. The four elevations of this house are almost identical except for the lean-to volumes arranged at different split-levels. Exterior walls have been made of Japanese cedar board with oil finished Douglas fir battens. Window frames are flush with the wood siding and of the same color so as to cause least distraction from the simple geometry of the elevations. Laid with weathered railroad sleepers, the garden path meanders through the rich natural woodlands.

Left The square and borderless *ryukyu* tatami mats in this Japanese room are typically usually used in martial arts studios. The square pit fireplace is for use in tea ceremonies. A top hung window is also typical of tearoom architecture. The lamp from Isamu Noguchi's Akari series is a harmonious blend of Japanese paper handcraft and modernist design.

Far left Openings on all sides of the house allow for cross breezes in hot humid weather. Wood frames have been designed to cover the aluminum frames of commercially available fly screens installed inside the sliding windows.

Left The plaited leather chaise lounge designed by Bruno Mathsson in 1941 provides for comfortable reading in the corner of the living room. Interior posts are wrapped with rattan to blend into the overall blonde wood palette. Vertical lines of the posts and mullions echo the trunks of larch trees outside.

Right top The owners are fond of Scandinavian design and worked with the architect to select pieces to furnish the house. Poul Hennigsen's PH 4/3 Louis Poulsen pendant hangs over the dining table, which was designed by the architect and built by Sobajima Katsumi. Borge Mogensen designed the beech dining chairs in 1947.

Right The sparse furnishings of the guest bedroom include a bed covered with a crisp linen cover and simple desk designed by the architect. All windows in the house are treated with fine bamboo roll screens.

Below The sofa, low table and sideboard were designed by the architect and built by Sobajima Katsumi for this house. The hearth has been finished with Shirakawa stone, and the fireplace selected from US manufacturer Majestic.

S HOUSE

This house is situated on a hill on a 12,300-square-meter plot well endowed with larch and acer trees, as well as giant ferns that grow in this moist hilly climate. The owner had seen the F house (also featured in this book) designed by Kosugi Hirohisa of Prop Position near his site, and asked him to design a glass house perched on top of this steep sloped site for his family. The ridge of the hill runs along the axis that connects Mount Asama and Mount Myogi, the two major mountain peaks around Karuizawa. The architect decided to design the house along this strong axis, with living spaces arranged on the north and south of this axis line with wide-open views on both sides. The goal was to create a special relationship with the scenery and to design a house where one can feel the sensation of being on a mountaintop. Since this area is full of beautiful timber homes, the exterior design also sought to be in keeping with the general character of the area.

This 146-square-meter house has been designed for a couple, their baby and pet dog. The narrow wood deck wrapping the south side of the house feels like theater seating for viewing the majestic views beyond. A larger terrace for alfresco dining is located on the east and is accessed from the kitchen and dining room. At the client's request, the kitchen and dining counter were designed to enable a person who is cooking to interact with people in the living room and on the terrace, and also to enjoy the view beyond. The counter that continues past the glass wall from the kitchen to the terrace helps bring the feeling of outdoors into the dining room. This 7-meter-long concrete counter was cast on site and sand-polished to a smooth, water-sealed finish with a toxin-free natural coating.

The mosaic glass-tiled bathroom is also a special part of this house. The large glass door swings fully open on pivot hinges to bring the great outdoors in, giving the bathroom a sanctuary-like feeling. Bathing outdoors at the *rotenburo* (outdoors hot spring bath) is a cherished Japanese desire.

The foundations and the ground floor, which houses the bathroom and utility room, are smaller and made of reinforced concrete, while timber structure has been deployed for the second floor guestroom. The larger volume that houses the living room and master bedroom is made of steel structure. Diagonal steel bracing at the entrance has been designed to counter lateral earthquake forces, and has been articulated in red color as a design element. Double-paned glass and floor heating using an oil boiler make the house comfortable during the cold winters of Karuizawa. All these thoughtful details have resulted in a simple, beautiful and functional vacation home that is easy to maintain and a pleasure to cook, dine and entertain in, making getting away from the everyday city stress truly a pleasure.

Previous spread The sharp edges of the terrace and its roof overhang articulate the clean lines of the house. Black stain from Xyladecor has been used on the exterior timber finish.

Far left The dining counter is fitted with an AEG halogen cooker so that the wife is able to cook at the table while conversing with her family or guests. The crisp black and white dining chairs are "Catifa 46" from Arper and have been designed by Lievore Atthere Molina.

Above Standing on the terrace, one gets the feeling of standing on the top of the mountain.

Left The 7-meter-long kitchen counter is extended outside on the terrace in one continuous line. Additional seating is provided by the sculptural built-in bench.

Left (from far to near) The Woodline series bathtub and basin, designed by Benedini Associates for the Italian manufacturer Agape, have a traditional *hinoki* wood tub feel to them but are made from molded plywood. The entrance hall, flooded with sunlight from the skylight above, acts as a pivot between the living and bedroom areas. This pivot function, seen in one continuous line from the entrance pathway into the house, has been articulated in the plan and elevations. The entrance hall is seen from the reverse side through the kitchen.

Below White and pale colors in all interior furnishings contrast with the dark exterior.

Below left The southern and eastern parts of the house are cantilevered off the lower floor and seem to be floating in the morning mist.

Above The long volume of the first floor gradually lifts off the slope and widens to the east, so that the terrace located at very eastern end of the house appears to be floating.

Left Wooden louvers help to control the sunlight and privacy in the house.

Below The Tufty Time modular sofa has been designed by Patricia Urquiola for B&B Italia. The warm yellow color of the sofa chair has been echoed in the cushions on the four-seater sofa.

Bottom The 7-meter-long kitchen counter also acts as a dining table and is extended outside on the terrace in one continuous line. High Frame Chairs on the terrace are designed by Meda from Cassina.

NIIGATA HOUSE

This suburban house has been conceived of as two horizontal layers that differ from each other in usage as well as their response to the surrounding landscape. Unlike most places in Japan, the landscape of rice fields in this part of Nishi-ku in Niigata Prefecture is not slated for redevelopment in the foreseeable future. Integrating this landscape presence into the interior was one of the main goals in the design of this house. Simplicity was another goal shared by the architect Ishii Daigo of Future-scape Architects and the client couple. The form of this house is made up of a long horizontal box with three smaller boxes placed on top of it in transverse direction. The sky is visible in between the top boxes, giving the structure a light and unassuming appearance appropriate to this flat landscape.

The lower layer of interconnected spaces stretches out in the east-west direction, and is designed for entertaining frequent guests. The windows and mirrors located on the long sides of this space emphasize its horizontality, a perception that is further enhanced by the lighting design. The rice fields in the background provide a distant but ever-present backdrop to all activities on this floor.

In contrast to the lower floor, the top layer is made up of three small individual huts, and accommodates the bedrooms and other private areas. These huts have openings on all four sides to ensure that light and wind from all directions provide constant awareness of nature. The placement of the huts is also staggered to further ensure the free flow of air in between them. The huts have been placed at 90 degrees to the lower floor and the paddy fields, with their longer sides aligned to the north-south direction. The owner couple and their two dogs spend much time here. The owner of the house is also an avid collector of designer furniture, which is displayed to an advantage in this spacious 195-square-meter home.

The architect surveyed traditional local materials and colors used for exterior walls in Niigata in an attempt to give the house a feeling of solidarity with its environs. Different materials and window placements have been used for each of the three huts on the second floor, so as to provide each one a different sort of interface with nature. Exterior of the western and eastern huts is finished with galvanized steel plates while the middle hut has cedar wood board siding stained black with Xyladecor. The dark tones of both materials appear similar at certain times of the day. However, the galvanized steel plates scatter light in all directions giving the hut an ephemeral appearance when it is sunny. This ephemeral quality has also been created in the interior of the middle hut by the use of galvanized steel walls, which contrast with its dark cedar exterior. This hut serves as the second floor foyer and also houses the utility room. Sleek, high-end radiators produced by PS Heating Systems provide heating throughout the residence.

The windows in each hut are also different. While the windows in the first hut are designed to present the scenery in a most natural way to the interior, those in the middle hut appear as picture frames from the inside and trim the scenery into neat rectangles. The carpeted floor in the eastern-most hut contrasts with its walls and ceiling, which have been conceived of as a reflection box made up of mirrors and glossy paint. As the landscape outside permeates in and is reflected by these interior surfaces, the boundary between virtual and real images is obscured, providing a surreal sensation of a unique place far away from ordinary life.

Previous spread Individual boxlike forms on the upper level of this house give a light and unassuming appearance appropriate to this flat landscape.

Above An exposed concrete facade encloses the courtyard and walkway leading to the entrance of the house. The cantilevered roof in front provides covered parking space.

Opposite top Considered one of the most significant chairs of twentieth-century design, the Eames lounge chair and ottoman are treasured items in this house. They are paired here with Isamu Noguchi's sculptural table and classic Arco lamp designed by the Castiglioni brothers. Custom-built wall-to-wall cabinetry keeps the open-plan kitchen free of clutter. Eames Shell chairs, upholstered in vivid orange, can be pulled up to the cast-on-site concrete counter. The chef's dream kitchen is equipped with a dual gas and electric convection oven. The audiovisual center is installed neatly on an adjacent wall.

Below (from left to right) The architect selected dark-toned materials with both reflective and absorptive surfaces for the exterior to produce contrasting effects in sunlight. The overlaying of different materials such as galvanized steel, polycarbonate sheets, mirrored surfaces, and black-stained *sugi* wood louvers wrapped around the middle hut create visual interest throughout the second floor.

Above Pivoting doors help make the narrow entrance hall feel spacious.

Above second and third The skylight installed in the middle hut allows plenty of natural light to flood down into the central staircase. Metal grills are fitted into part of the floor to allow the floor below to get natural light. Stairs leading to the second floor guest bedroom wing are seen in the background. The top of the stairs is seen in the third righ picture above.

Left to right The galvanized steel walls scatter light in all directions giving the hut an ephemeral appearance when it is sunny. Golden rice fields in the autumn sun are visible from all the rooms in the house. A small basin has been installed for convenient use at the top of the stairs.

Above far right Located in the center of the spacious maple floored living/dining area, the galvanized steel staircase reflects the aesthetic principles of the house.

Right The living area is designed as one long horizontal space so that movements of its inhabitants are always parallel to the backdrop of the landscape. The stairs to the guest bedroom in the eastern-most hut are concealed behind a freestanding mirrored closet. Seen reflected in this mirror are more Eames classics and the popular Tolomeo lamp designed by Michele de Lucci.

Far left The staircase leads up to the middle hut that is surfaced entirely with galvanized steel plates. Seen at the top of the stairs behind sliding doors, finished with galvanized steel on the outer and shina veneer on the inner side, is the library in the master bedroom wing in the western hut.

Above (from top to bottom) Built from cherry wood blocks, Frank Lloyd Wright's Taliesin lamp sits in the corner of the master bedroom floor, which is surfaced with modest plywood with waxed *shina* wood veneer, echoing mid-century modernism. All white finishes define the bathroom. The house is designed to help the residents stay creative, and playful touches such as those shown here echo that theme.

Right top The silhouettes of the three huts are articulated against the open sky.

Right The bathroom faces the back courtyard on the ground floor. The architect designed the cast-concrete pedestal counter fitted with a Vola basin and folding shutters that slide across the windows to open a vanity mirror or privacy when needed.

FOUR-IN-ONE HOUSE

The deconstructive design of this house plays with the motif of a primal house seeking to harmonize a relatively large structure into a neighborhood crowded with small homes. The site is located beside a tree-lined promenade along the Gake River in Adachi-ku on the outskirts of Tokyo. Typical of many suburbs, the agricultural land here was subdivided into small lots and built over by individual owners in a relatively haphazard manner. The owner for this house bought four consecutive lots to make up the 600 square meters needed to build a 400-square-meter home for himself, his wife, two children and their pet dog.

The architects Takayasu Shigekazu and Imazu Shuhei of Architecture Lab were selected via a design competition. They proposed three alternatives to show their design capabilities and engage the owner in the design process. The exterior of the house looks like four independent houses in a row, each with its own steep roof pitched at a different angle. The pitch is exaggerated as much as possible, except at the entrance where it has been kept low in deference to the street scale. The length of the pitched roofs was limited to four meters, the distance of the structural walls on the sides of each "house." These roofs also create a dramatic interior space, which is traversed by an axial hallway that runs across the four houses, and from which other spaces emanate. The double-height volume of this hallway provides a sense of orientation and order in the house while uniting its two levels. The sense of depth along the hallway is enhanced by the nine different shades of oil stain on the ash wood floor. These have been graded from the front of the house toward the back. The floor of each one of the four independent houses is also stained a different color, while the transition piece between each is a mixture of the two adjacent colors.

A water table was discovered a meter below the ground at this riverside site, which was formerly a rice paddy, with bedrock another 54 meters below. This prompted the architects to design a raft foundation, referred to as the "Columbus" technique in Japan. Soil equal to the total weight of the house was removed from the site to avoid additional load on the soil. The house rests on a 1.5-meter-deep raft foundation, which is a protective measure against flooding from the nearby river and ground liquefaction during large earthquakes.

Due to the excessive water content of this area, the governing drainage codes are stringent. The architects have installed circular pipes with perforated covers that catch leaves from the surrounding trees and drain water at the gutters where the pitched roofs meet. The water is allowed to fall naturally onto the ground and drained through gravel-filled trenches.

The concrete structure has been finished on both exterior and interior with a high-tech waterproof ceramic insulation paint that was originally developed for space shuttles. The paint is photosensitive and wards off UV rays, and causes dirt particles to slide off the surface.

The expansive feeling inside the house is retained by treating all storage areas as built-in furniture. While black-stained *nara* wood veneer covers the kitchen, entrance storage cubes, and the audiovisual center in the living room, all other built-in furniture has been treated as walls and finished with white urethane-based paint.

Previous spread The lighting design took into consideration the night views of the house, and effectively highlights the varying roof pitches. Though they may appear random, each window has been designed to crop or highlight a particular view of the garden, sky or foliage.

Left Bold functional cabinets define various areas of the living space without interrupting the dramatic flow of space. The cabinet in the foreground has been designed as the audiovisual center. The sofa is from Casa Milano and ottoman/table cubes are from HH style. The dining room and kitchen are located behind the farthest cabinet.

Right The modern Japanese room is fitted with square borderless *ryukyu* tatami mats. Shoji screens open to dramatic views of the garden. There are four traditional gardens in the house, cropped views of which can be seen from several rooms.

Below The countertop and inside of the double island kitchen is faced with hairline finish stainless steel. One island houses the sink and dishwasher while the other is fitted with a refrigerator and a teppan grill.

Left The ceiling, made of exposed concrete, is uninterrupted by ceiling lights or other mechanical fixtures. The clean detailing is the result of the formwork that was prepared to exactly fit the dimensions of each ceiling plane.

Near right A lacquered shelf in the Japanese room is suspended over pebbles by a single charcoal smoke–stained bamboo pillar in the tokonoma alcove. The handwoven bamboo Hizuki floor lamp is designed by Marei.

Far right Surfaced with white pebbles, the modernized "contemplation garden," designed by the owner and the family gardener, features a meticulously pruned maple tree, an island planted with *Ophiopogon japonicus* (commonly known as lily turf or mondo grass), and a composition of natural rocks. The combination of these elements is traditionally meant to symbolize heaven, earth and man.

Below The sense of depth along this hallway is enhanced by the nine different shades of oil stain on the ash wood floor.

Above As in this children's room, window openings add to the spacious feeling within the house. Eight different types of window frames have been used, including those that fold, tilt, slide across each other, slide into pockets, and are hinged. This was a conscious design choice by the architects to give each window a functional identity.

Above right Carpeted in black, the second floor mezzanine is used for a children's play area. This space also leads to a library, personal gym and a bathroom facing a balcony that is fitted with a Jacuzzi tub.

Right The spacious stone-paved shower area opens onto a balcony.

Second right The walls of the luxurious Japanese bathroom have been finished with fragrant *hiba* wood while the slatted wooden floors are made of *hinoki* wood, favored for its subtle fragrance. *Koyamaki* wood was selected for the soaking tub for its durability.

Third right All mechanical equipment such as air conditioners is embedded in built-in furniture or the floors.

Far right Situated in a secluded wing, the master bedroom is flanked by a large deck on one side and a small garden on the other. Archimoon Soft lamps designed by Phillipe Starck provide bedside reading light.

MEJIRO HOUSE

How do you pour eternity into a tea cup? This question is as relevant in tea ceremony as in the practice of architecture in Japan. Concepts for making eyes travel beyond the edge of a hanging scroll or the surface of a tiny floor to provide a feeling of expansiveness have been perfected over hundreds of years. Nowhere is such innovation needed more than in the design of small homes in Tokyo, where real estate prices continue to be among the highest in the world.

This house in Mejiro is an example of how small spaces with clean lines and meticulous detailing can result in an inspiring environment even in a cluttered neighborhood. Located in busy residential area in Tokyo, the site for the 207- square-meter house faces two private roads on its south and west, with the street on the south culminating in a dead end a short distance from the house. All streets in this area are packed with houses on both sides, each struggling for a measure of privacy for its inhabitants as well as some sunlight. The strict sunlight regulations and height restrictions necessary to make such areas inhabitable also result in challenges for the architects here. While some houses turn their back on the street with a solid facade devoid of windows, other houses have small windows on the street, with shutters and curtains that stay permanently drawn. However, the client for this house asked the architects Mori Kiyotoshi and Kawamura Natsuko of MDS Studio to create a feeling of openness as well as privacy for his house. His request also included a double height living room filled with light. The architects started the design process by trying to thoroughly understand the site, and decided to design a house that would add something positive to the streetscape while fulfilling the design brief of the owner.

The solution was to make the house open and relatively transparent at the street level, while lowering the level of the living areas below and above the site-line from the street, thus reinventing the usual exterior-foyer-interior continuum. The house in fact acts as a visual relief on its two streets that are otherwise closed on both sides. A passerby can see right across the house through the glass walls. The only room visible from the street is the art gallery for the art collector owner, which adds to the positive experience of the street.

From the entrance level, an airy staircase takes residents down to the living area and up to the bedroom level. The double-height living room does not feel like a basement because it is has open patios on either side, and is filled with daylight from the tall windows and skylights. The breeze from outside can flow through the house, and the diagonal views of the clean minimalist spaces on various levels provide a sense of spaciousness in the house. The views of the blue sky during the day and the starry night, as well as the changing colors and angles of light with different seasons, time and weather, make this a comfortable space. The architects believe that design should respond to the absolute elements of light, wind and time as well as the individual needs of the owners.

Previous spread The open patios on either side of the living room provide a sense of openness and natural ventilation. The wood flooring on the patio is at the same level as the trowel finished concrete on the inside to enhance the feeling of continuity between the two spaces. The Dadone modular sofa and Solo table are designed by Antonio Citterio and manufactured by B&B Italia.

Left A variety of concrete finishes have been used throughout the house. The formwork for the concrete on the street facade seen on the right of the entrance was made of cedar board. The narrow glass case on the left was custom designed to display the owner's collection of the coveted edition of "50 Artist Toys" produced by Visionaire, the much talked about New York–based multi-format publication that melds fashion and art.

Above The texture of the hammer-finished concrete on the staircase wall shows off to an advantage as it is washed with light coming from the skylight above the staircase. Poured concrete has been used for the floor finish.

Above left The flat screen TV has been neatly hung in the wall alcove of the living room. Although it is situated on the level below the street, the living room does not feel like it is in the basement as it is flooded with natural light and has open patios on either side.

Far left The living room is seen through the glass wall of the wood decked patio located next to the kitchen. The ledge provided for inside the living room has been continued as a bench in the exterior patio. A portrait of Madonna photographed by Mario Testino, one of the fashionista's most sought after photographers, sits on the ledge.

Near left As in traditional Japan, an area of slatted wooden flooring for bathing before entering the soaking tub has been provided in this bathroom.

Above The cool colors of the exposed concrete in the kitchen and dining room area have been balanced with the warm tones of the wood flooring and kitchen counter.

Left While the house opens to views of the art gallery from the other street level, the relatively closed facade on this street also provides a measure of openness to the narrow street.

Right Diagonal views across rooms and various levels enhance a sense of expansive space in this house. The bridge housing the entrance gallery space is seen above the living room.

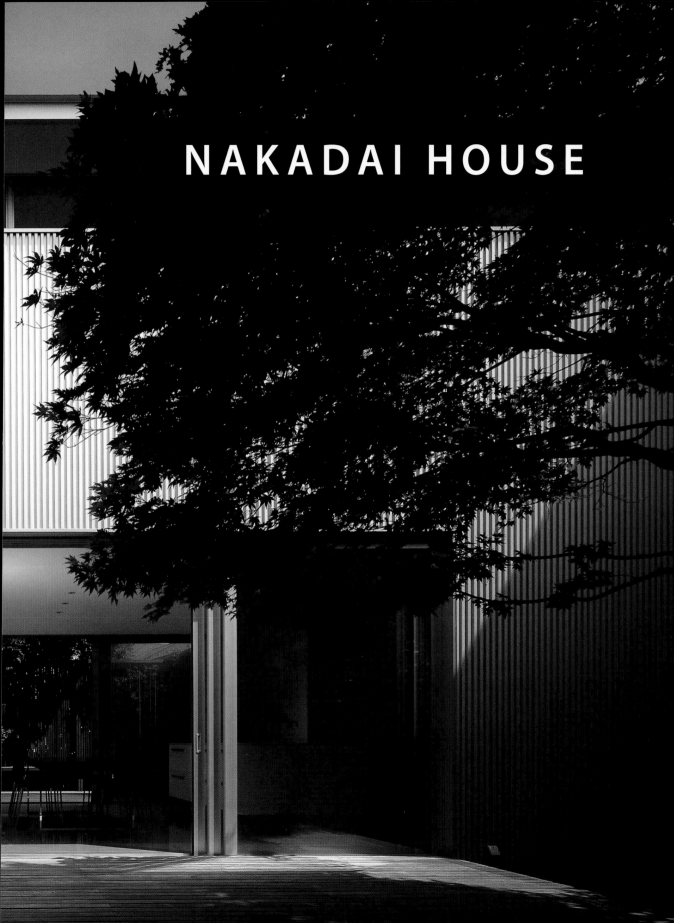

NAKADAI HOUSE

This home on a small lot in the suburbs of Tsurumi-ku in Yokohama succeeds in creating a quiet oasis of stillness amid a chaotic neighborhood of small houses. It achieves this feat by keeping the built-up area to the minimum needed, while creating two generous decks on the ground floor on either side of the living room, and another two on the second floor for the master bedroom. Each room in the house thus has access to an open deck surrounded by greenery, imparting a feeling of spaciousness. Its location on a hill gives these decks the advantage of good breeze and open views.

This 163–square-meter house is designed for a couple and their daughter. The wife, Omori Midori, works as an in-house architect for a large urban redevelopment firm and had a clear idea of the architectural concept of her house. She wanted the plan to consist of two simple boxlike forms arranged perpendicular to each other, and searched for another architect to help her realize this idea. She soon decided on a creative collaboration with Nakagame Kiyonobu+Nakagame Kiyonobu Architect and Associates, who helped her to further articulate the exterior of the two intersecting boxes in galvanized steel and wood. This idea of smartly contrasting colors has also been carried into the interior, where the light-colored walls are set off by flooring made of aluminum panels in the living and bedroom while dark stained wood has been used for the entrance. She asked for the walls to be finished with mat finish and neutral colors to enable her to decorate and redecorate over years to come. The interior spaces have been kept uncluttered. A frosted glass wall at the end of the living room, as well as the perforated hanging screen at the entrance, define these areas in a subtle way without impinging of the flow of space.

Constructed of timber, the structural system of the house consists of 120-x-60-millimeter rectangular laminated timber columns that are embedded within the walls from the ground floor up. From the second floor on, these columns act as vertical cantilevers in transmitting the weight of the roof as well as lateral forces onto the flat bars at the top of the long ribbon windows. Flooring has been made of 1.2-x-1.2- meter aluminum sheets of 2 millimeter thickness. Aluminum was selected over the initially planned stone flooring by Omori in order to reduce the dead weight of the house and consequently the additional cost that would have been necessary for the foundation. After searching for alternative lightweight materials, the owner decided on aluminum due to its aesthetic qualities. Aluminum can also easily be produced in large size panels of up to 2.4 x 2.4 meters and installed with minimal joints.

Since aluminum is also an efficient thermal conductor it helps with the floor heating that has been provided in the entire home. Contrary to the expectation that metal flooring would be cold and hard, the anodized aluminum panels gently reflect sunlight, adding to the feeling of softness in the interior. The neutral, lightweight and precise characteristics of aluminum also reflect the personality of the homeowner.

Previous spread Large decks form an important part of the living space of this house. The structural system of the house has been designed so that the peripheral walls carry the entire load, leaving the interior spaces unobstructed by columns or partitions.

Right The living and dining rooms in the first floor are flanked by courtyards on the south as well as the north side and are flooded with light. Charles sofas in the living room have been designed by Antonio Citterio for B&B Italia. The coffee table is made from an old Indian door and was purchased at a New York auction. *Wenge* wood has been used in the entrance hall flooring seen in the foreground. A wenge wood slab has also been placed on top of aluminum table legs from Muji to form the desk.

Far left On this credenza, elegant glass candle stands purchased in Prague sit alongside funky bookends and a painting by the owner's son.

Middle left An antique Chinese window frame from the Ch'ing Period (1644–1795) is used in the entrance hall as a partition screen.

Near left A transparent glass wall separates the staircase from the living room without interupting the flow of space.

Below The floor heating rapidly warms up the aluminum floor in the winters and is a pleasure to walk on barefoot. The couple's daughter also enjoyed crawling on it as a baby.

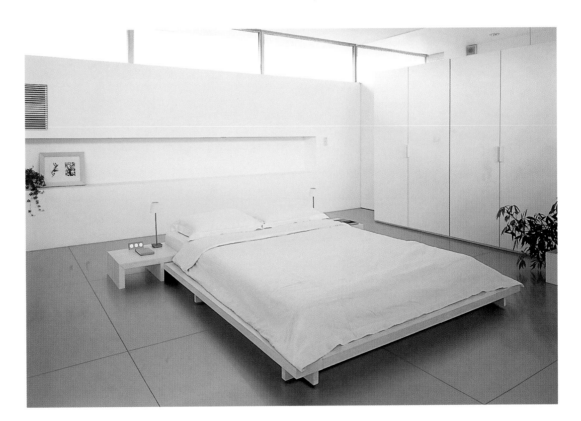

Top The thick aluminum mullions of the oversized double-glazed windows appear surprisingly unobtrusive and also relate to the aluminum flooring. The dining room features Lia dining chairs designed by Roberto Barbieri from Zanotta and an Athos dining table designed by Paolo Piva from B&B Italia.

Above Windows in the main bedroom have been located high enough to provide privacy from the neighbors, while allowing sunlight to come in. The owners believe in owning just the minimum in terms of clothing and other belongings, so only a few closets and storage spaces were necessary in the house.

Above The sleek yet functional kitchen counter was made to the owner's design by Italian kitchen company Monte.

Above right This same wall is seen from inside of the house flanked by two glass walls located in the entrance hall. The ribbon windows of the master bedroom are seen on the right wall.

Right Surrounded by lush greenery, the house exudes a feeling of spaciousness as well as privacy. The exterior wall plated with galvanized steel wall juts out from the building providing privacy to the entrance area from the neighboring house.

F HOUSE

This shared vacation home is located in Karuizawa, a holiday destination in Nagano Prefecture so popular with Tokyoites that it is often referred to as the 24th ward to Tokyo's 23 wards. The house was commissioned by two IT professionals who wanted a weekend place for their families. Its location in a valley in a vacation home area gives it a good view of city lights as well as deciduous trees that abound in Karuizawa.

The program developed jointly by the owners and the architect Kosugi Hirohisa of Prop Position called for well-defined public and private spaces to allow the two families to share the house while still affording some measure of privacy. While the boundaries between private and public space can often be blurred in a single-family house, they had to be carefully considered in this situation. Public spaces have been designed so that they are flexible and can be used in a variety of ways as needed by the occupants. For example, the living/dining room and the bar are independent spaces, which may also be used as work spaces by simply bringing in laptop computers.

Although most people go to Karuizawa to immerse themselves in the natural environs they miss in the city, the owners of this house wanted to strike a balance between urban and resort living. The bar and the 120-inch DVD screen with a surround-sound system in the living room ensure that the owners do not have to miss such amenities while on vacation. However, this 181-square-meter house also has generous outdoor spaces and picture windows that help the occupants enjoy the abundant natural beauty of Karuizawa.

A steel frame structure has been used for the house. The boxlike forms of the bar and the main bathroom with its private terrace have been articulated on the exterior of the house. Windows have been designed to frame the views of the majestic trees on and around the site. Louvers all across the terrace outside the bedrooms allow for control of light and privacy. This enables users to experience the sound of rain and breezes outside while controlling the level of light and privacy desired. Electric floor heating has been provided in all rooms, while a wood-burning stove adds to the ambiance of relaxation in the living room.

Playful elements add to the special feeling in this house. The kitchen is housed in a cylindrical space while the living/dining room has a café feel to it. The original idea in the program of a study on the second floor morphed into a private bar that can be used as a study/work area as needed. Its private staircase access from outside ensures that late night guest do not disturb the children. The bar as well as the loft space for additional guests have been conceived of as floating volumes in a double-height space. The bar has a curved ceiling rendered in deep blue. All these details add up to a delightful house that make this house a true weekend retreat.

Previous spread and near left The 7.5-x-2.7-meter picture window helps bring the feel of the mountain inside the house. The 5-meter-wide terrace seen beyond the window acts as an extension of the living/dining room for alfresco dining and entertaining. The Joseph Hoffman Kubus leather sofa in the living room is a modern cubist classic.

Far left The boxlike forms of the bar and the main bathroom with its private terrace have been articulated on the exterior of the house. Windows have been designed to frame the views of the majestic trees on and around the site.

Below The bar has independent access from outside for late night guests. The bar counter is made of 3-meter-long solid piece of oil stained *aba* wood.

Below left The second floor is accessed by an elegant steel staircase.

Above Louvers are provided in all the bedrooms to allow inhabitants to control light and privacy.

Far left The living room flooring is a virtually warp-free wood product called EW8, developed by Japanese manufacturer AD World. Harvested from plantations in New Zealand and Australia, *radiata* pine is sliced and saturated with natural cellulose polymers that radically harden and stain the pinewood.

Middle left Furniture and the dining counter have been custom built in this playful kitchen.

Near left The bathroom has a full glass wall that leads to a private open court. Continuing the floor level and the material of the bathroom to the court gives the bathroom an expansive feeling. A blower-type Jacuzzi bath from Jaxson Corporation has been installed in this luxurious bathroom. Bathroom fixtures and plumbing equipment were selected for easy maintenance during winter months when the house is not in use.

Left The living room and staircase is seen from the large terrace.

Below The furnishings on the 5-meter-wide red cedar wood clad terrace include Vico Magestretti Maui chairs paired with a glass table.

Right A steel frame structure has been used for the house. This allowed for parts of the second floor to be supported on columns to provide ample outdoor space on the ground floor, and to articulate the various spaces inside.

HOVER HOUSE

This house is located in the part of Eastern Hiroshima that is still full of greenery, paddy fields and bamboo groves. Because of a national park and a flood pond nearby, the site is in a specially regulated urban zone with restrictions on the density of houses that may be built there. The client chose this site for its surroundings, and wanted a house with maximum opportunities for enjoying the scenery.

The design of this 185-square-meter house followed the shape of the site and resulted in a boomerang-shaped plan with wings extending to the east and west. All the rooms have been arranged around the large southern deck with a great view of the flood pond. This terrace also serves as a seamless extension of the living space.

The height difference between the two roads adjoining the site has been used to ensure privacy of the glass fronted living areas and the deck. The approach to the house is from the higher end of the north road, which results in the level of the house and the deck being about 1.5 meters above the lower south road.

An innovative structural system akin to assembling sticks and building blocks has been adopted for the house. Rather than using a concrete foundation that would trap moisture in this humid environment, architects Nakazono Tetsuya of Naf Architecture & Design and Nawa Kenji+nawakenjim chose a system that would allow the wind to pass through. Since the site was a former paddy field, a traditional foundation would have had to be dug down below a meter of soft soil on this site. Winged stakes were instead used as piles to hold up the house, also enabling it to be raised by 1.3 meters above the uneven terrain. This solution also has the added advantage of keeping the option open to return the site to its original use as a paddy field—a thoughtful consideration for a home in a fragile eco-system in a country with shrinking available land. This system of using structural posts is a modern version of traditional Japanese construction method where wooden posts resting on small stone bases supported farm houses.

The super structure is made up of slender factory-made steel posts and beams and concrete slabs, earning the house a nickname of "Stick House," which were welded on site, expediting the construction process. The 60-millimeter-diameter round steel bars used as posts cause minimum disruption to the views seen from the interior. The beams are made of 40 x 230 millimeter flat bars.

Although new materials and technological developments today make it easy to use fancy structural forms, the architect wanted to use basic materials and a simple form for the house where functionality, structure and materials would be articulated. Avoiding the use of temporary building materials and wasteful building practices was also a conscious decision by the owner and the architects. All construction materials and processes were expressed in the finished product instead of being covered over with other finishes. For example, steel molds used for casting concrete slabs were left in place to provide connections for other structural members as they were built up.

The design of this house makes year-round use of the natural environment to keep the interior of the house at a comfortable temperature. All rooms are warmed by plentiful sunshine coming in through south-facing glass walls during winter. Walls facing away from the deck on the north are made of concrete, completely closed off, and lined with storage closets for additional insulation. During summer, the deck is made comfortable by the air that rises up in between the joints of the wood slat flooring, having been cooled by the contact with the cobblestones underneath the deck. The pool on the deck terrace is filled from a well underneath the floor.

In a relatively long structure such as this, it is usually difficult to design an energy efficient HVAC system. However, what would normally be a disadvantage has been turned into an advantage in this house by placing all mechanical equipment under the floor slab. Hot water heaters are placed underneath the bathrooms and the kitchen, and fan coil units placed near the air conditioners to minimize loads. Plumbing pipes are exposed underneath the house, making it easy to service them. Moveable wooden panels have been used as walls, providing easy access to equipment behind them.

Previous spread The deck is lifted 1.5 meters above the south road and has a 1-meter-high railing, which provides a good measure of privacy in this semi-rural setting. It offers a good view of the paddy fields and bamboo groves around and is also the main play space for the three children in this family, their English bulldog and a pet rabbit.

Above The light and easily transported lath net usually employed for applying the first plaster coat for walls was pinned to wood stiffeners and used as a mold for pouring concrete walls. When concrete is poured into such molds, the liquidity and weight of the concrete give it a wavelike pattern, which has been left exposed.

Top right The client purchased the sofa and dining chairs from Bo Concept. The coffee table was designed by Isamu Noguchi. Nakazono, the architect for this house, designed the dining table and the table in the study.

Near right The main bathroom and a study are the only two spaces located on the large roof terrace.

Middle right While the exterior of the house is made of industrial materials, wooden finishes make the interior spaces warm and inviting.

Far right The house has been designed in a boomerang shape around the central deck.

Top The house has been designed around the large deck with timber flooring.

Above Bathing in the sun-filled bathroom on the roof terrace feels like floating on a sea of paddy fields

Right top The metal portions of the exterior stairs, handrails, and garage door have been zinc-plated and treated with phosphoric acid to make them weather resistant.

Right The normal practice in reinforced concrete construction is to use cheap lauan wood for formwork, dispose of it after construction, and then finish the walls with a finer wood or other facing material. However the 1-x-5-meter pieces of laminated spruce used as formwork for pouring concrete slabs for the ceiling here were left in place as the final interior finish. Such methods used in this house helped make the construction process friendly to the environment by reducing waste.

AO HOUSE

Previous spread The living and dining areas of the house have been located on the second floor to get the best views of the forest through the floor-to-ceiling mullion-less glazing. Classic modern furniture from the middle of the twentieth century was selected for these areas. The daybed PK80 was designed by Poul Kjaerholm in 1957, and is now in the collection of the Museum of Modern Art in New York.

Above The only way to go from one room to the other is to pass through the open courtyard or the patio, thus allowing inhabitants to connect with nature several times during the course of the day.

Right The house sits like a bridge on top of a valley, with a staircase that extends from the entrance, under the house and onto this wooden deck.

Far right The wooden deck at the lower level has been built around the existing trees that were carefully preserved.

Located in the green hills of Chichibu about two hours from Tokyo, this house was designed by architect Oshio Shoji of UA Architects Tokyo Office to help the inhabitants develop an intimate sense of nature. While one can enjoy the scenery of the distant mountains from many places, the clients wanted to also enrich the inside of their home and daily lives with the beauty of the natural surroundings in Chichibu. This goal has been achieved by arranging all the rooms of the house around a large open courtyard, a cubic volume that steps down to provide a passage under the house and out to the deck surrounded with trees and to the stream and forest beyond. The only way to go from one room to another is to pass through this open courtyard. This circulation pattern enables the inhabitants to experience fresh air and the sound of rushing water from the nearby brook several times during the course of a day.

The 211-square-meter house has been conceptualized on two platforms, each one with its own personality. Private areas with bedrooms are located on the lower level, where the essential aesthetics is that of exposed concrete. The directionality of the walls here focuses the views toward the windows that overlook the saw tooth oak trees in the backyard. The owner had requested that these beautiful trees that take up nearly half of the site on the north be preserved.

In contrast to concrete walls at the lower level, glass walls surround the upper level to provide panoramic views of the nearby treetops and distant mountains in all four directions. The inhabitants can thus enjoy a different view of nature from each level.

A thin wall, reinforced concrete shell structure, also called "Tunnel Structure," has been used for the house. Reinforced concrete walls also make up the exterior facades. The concrete surface of these walls is imprinted with the pattern of the vertical cedar formwork used for casting the concrete. This verticality has been inspired by the trees that surround the house.

The client and the architect both share a preference for modern simplicity, which is reflected in the minimalist aesthetics of this house and the architect's selection of furniture. Floor to ceiling glass walls with slender frames, and the continuation of the interior flooring to the outside, promote a feeling of continuity between the interior and exterior spaces.

The design of air-conditioning in the living space on the second floor underscores the fine balance of functionality and aesthetics sought in this house. Since exposed air-conditioning equipment would clutter up the interior, it was installed under the floor with outlets located in the floor along the windows, as well as inside the walls. All equipment is covered with industrial grade louver boards.

Above This covered patio provides a perfect place to view the majestic landscape around the house. The sculptural Axent chaise lounge was designed by Giuseppe Vigano and has been distributed by Ivano Redaelli.

Left The PK24 Wicker chaise lounge has been designed by Poul Kjaerholm and produced by Fritz Hansen.

Right All surfaces on the second floor have been finished with marble, glass, metal or exposed concrete.

Far right All spaces of the house have been placed around the large open courtyard, a cubic volume that steps down to provide a passage under the house and onto the deck with trees, and to the stream and forest beyond.

Above Exposed concrete walls in this bedroom as well as other places in this house have been imprinted with the pattern of the vertical cedar formwork used for casting them. This verticality has been inspired by the trees that surround the house.

Above left The design of the shoji paper screens in the tatami rooms is unusual and innovative in that they slide into the middle of the wall, leaving the glass corners free.

Left All the furniture in the living dining area is minimalist in concept. The lounge chair PK22 in the foreground was designed by Poul Kjaerholm in 1956. The glass table PK61 was designed by Poul Kjaerholm in 1955 and is typical of his table designs which all tend to be square, have glass tops and stainless steel bases. The low cupboard on the right and dining table named Table88 were designed by Maarten Van Severen. The leather dining chairs are called Extra Chair, designed by Fabien Baron and distributed by Cappellini.

E HOUSE

While the design of most houses in this book is driven by practical and aesthetic considerations that have remained unchanged for hundreds of years, this house represents something closer to the funky new *manga* and *anime* culture of Japan and feels more like a set from a video game than a house. The building has an attitude, which the architect refers to as its subtle expression of communication with the neighborhood. Slightly shifting the angle of one's chair, or turning eyes away from others upon entering a crowded café, are other examples of such gestures of communication in every day life. This house makes its statement in the crowded city by its angular form, but does not cut off its neighbors completely. The architect sought to design this house based more upon such considerations than on cerebral logic.

The owner operates a company that rents trendy new fashion clothing from Japan and abroad to the entertainment industry. Since he feels that most Japanese architects design boring houses that all look rectangular and white, he chose Fukushima Katsuya of FT architects precisely because he had no prior experience of designing houses, and challenged him to think out of the box.

This 101-square-meter house is located in Setagaya, one of the most densely built-up areas in Tokyo where securing privacy is a main challenge. The interior of the house has been enveloped by an exterior screen/wall that twists and bends in various directions. The inspiration for this screen came from the traditional Japanese cloth called *furoshiki* that is used for wrapping various things without altering their shape. The angular walls and screens that are lifted up from the ground were not the result of deliberate manipulation of construction materials, techniques, or logical planning, but rather in spontaneous response to actual site circumstances, derived through experimentation with study models.

The owner wanted to live in a space that is not a house but more like a studio or a factory. This and many other requests from the owner were studied carefully and incorporated in the design in a nonjudgmental fashion. The entire house was then wrapped around with walls and screens like a furoshiki that does not question its contents.

This house is designed in terms of zones rather than rooms for a family of three who all love taking *ofuro* baths. Since the bath is the most important ritual for this family, the two bathrooms were located where they would receive maximum sunshine. The remaining rooms such as the studio, the dining room and bedrooms were arranged around the bathrooms. Separations between the rooms have been kept fuzzy and tentative, and defined with steps, level differences, and screens of cloth or other translucent materials. Conventions such the separation of the bathtub from the bedroom have been spurned. The only way to reach the second floor is by walking through the main bathroom.

A steel frame structure has been adopted for the house since the building site is narrow and the architect wanted to use the least possible space for the walls and the structure. Computer modeling was undertaken in order to arrive at the most slender columns possible. The result is a structure of 100-x-100-millimeter H-type steel columns and beams. The floor design of the second floor bedroom is also innovative in that a unified structure using steel plates above a concrete sub-layer has been used. This has enabled a 100-millimeter-thick floor to span about five meters without any intermediate column and beams.

The house has been designed to minimize the use of mechanical equipments. Natural ventilation and lighting has been used as much as possible by placing windows on opposite walls of a room. A hot water–based radiant heating system has been employed due to the open configuration of the rooms. However, the architect considers the lack of unnecessary spaces, equipment or things in the house the biggest energy saving measure.

Previous spread and above The exterior of this house has been wrapped with screens made up of expanded metal of the sort used for guardrails, and permeable polyester mesh made for gymnasiums. In places these materials have been bent or piled as if they were made of cloth.

Left From the bed/bathroom at the guest zone on the third floor, the space cascades down like an origami paper creation. Origami paper was in fact used for making study models.

Top The furnishing mix in the studio ranges from off-the-shelf inexpensive fabrics and furniture to classic signature works like La Chaise by Charles & Ray Eames and Basculant by Le Corbusier.

Above This view from the ofuro bath underlines the owner and the architect's belief that by adjusting the peripheral edges between the city and house, stresses caused by the densely populated surroundings can be managed. The city is admitted into the house at will through gaps between the screens that envelop the house.

Right The use of common materials in an uncommon way is one of the fun features of this house. Translucent curtains have been used to define spaces and uses instead of solid walls.

Above The spaces in this house flow into each other and are loosely defined with level changes or partial temporary curtains.

Right Taking ofuro baths is an important ritual for this family, so the bathrooms are located to receive maximum sunshine and views. This bathroom finished with vibrant turquoise border tiles looks out on a small garden enclosed by polyester screen fastened on a metal framework.

ARCHITECTS

We have adopted the Japanese way of presenting names, with the family name first.

1. Ashihara Hiroko

office Ashihara Hiroko Design Office

5F 5-5-7 Shirokanedai, Minato-ku, Tokyo 108-0071

phone/fax +81 3 5789 4842 / +81 3 5789 4843

e-mail/url info@ashiharahiroko.com / http://ashiharahiroko.com

selected projects

2001 Ristorante Hamasaki (Minato-ku, Tokyo)

2002 CARDIF (Shibuya-ku, Tokyo)

2003 Hiroo House (Minato-ku, Tokyo)

2004 Diana Garden Daikanyama (Meguro-ku, Tokyo)

Takanawa House (Minato-ku, Tokyo)

2005 Muromachi Wakuden (Sakaimachi, Kyoto City)

Shirokane House (Minato-ku, Tokyo)

Bancho Park House (Chiyoda-ku, Tokyo)

Mountain Villa (Chubu Region)

2006 Minami Azabu House (Minato-ku, Tokyo)

The Tower Osaka Model Room (Fukushima-ku, Osaka)

Ginza Aster (Chuo-ku, Tokyo)

2007 Genyadana Hamadaya Tokyo Midtown (Minato-ku, Tokyo)

2. Fukushima Katsuya

office FT architects

5-22-3-305 Komazawa Setagaya-ku Tokyo, Japan 154-0012

phone/fax +81 3 3410 8950

e-mail katsuyafu@yahoo.co.jp

selected projects/awards

2004 Nagoya C Office Building (Yotomi-cho, Aichi Prefecture)

JIA (Japan Institute of Architects) Best Young Architect Award

2006 American Wood Design of the Year

JID (Japan Interior Designer's Association) Award

Biennial, Interior Space Prize

AIJ (Architectural Institute of Japan) Award

3. Fuse Shigeru

office fuse-atelier

6-19-6 Makuhari-nishi, Mihama-ku, Chiba 261-0026, Chiba Prefecture

phone/fax +81 43 296 1828 / +81 43 296 1829

e-mail/url fuse@fuse-a.com / www.fuse-a.com

selected projects

1999 House in Makuhari-nishi (Chiba, Chiba Prefecture)

2001 House in Minami-aoyama (Minato-ku, Tokyo)

2002 House in Hanasaki (Narashino, Chiba Prefecture)

2003 House in Sekihara (Adachi-ku, Tokyo)

2004 House in Natsumi (Funabashi, Chiba Prefecture)

House in Yakuendai (Funabashi, Chiba Prefecture)

House in Nakamachi (Setagaya-ku, Tokyo)

House in Nishiogi-kita (Suginami-ku, Tokyo)

House in Asahi (Asahi, Chiba Prefecture)

2006 House in Hasama (Funabashi, Chiba Prefecture)

House in Myouden (Ichikawa, Chiba Prefecture)

House in Mizue (Edogawa-ku, Tokyo)

2007 House in Hirata (Ichikawa, Chiba Prefecture)

House in Midorigaoka (Sanbugun, Chiba Prefecture)

4. Hasegawa Go

office Hasegawa Go & Associates

5F Gaien Bldg. 2-18-7 Jingumae, Shibuya-ku, Tokyo 150-00011

phone/fax +81 3 3403 0336/ +81 3 3403 0337

e-mail/url hsgwg@ybb.ne.jp /www.hsgwg.com

selected projects/awards

2005 SD Review Kajima Award

2006 House in Sakuradai (Yokkaichi, Mie Prefecture)

House in Gotanda (Shinagawa-ku, Tokyo)

2007 Tokyo Gas House Design Competition 1st Prize

Tokyo Residence Award Gold Prize

5. Horibe Yasushi

office Horibe Yasushi Architect & Associates

601, 4-5-17 Kohinata, Bunkyo-ku, Tokyo 112-0006

phone/fax +81 3 3942 9080 /+81 3 3942 9087

e-mail/url horibe@yf7.so-net.ne.jp/www012.upp.so-net.ne.jp/horibe

selected projects

1995 House in Satsuma (Satsuma, Kagoshima Prefecture)

Dr. Norichika Maehara Memorial Museum (Satsuma, Kagoshima Prefecture)

1997 House at Akiya (Yokosuka, Kanagawa Prefecture)

1998 House in Omiya (Omiya-ku, Saitama)

House in Izu-kougen (Ito, Shizuoka Prefecture)

1999 House in Hibarigaoka (Higasikurume-shi, Tokyo)

2000 House in Yakushima (Yaku-cho Kumage, Kagoshima Prefecture)

2001 Gallery in Ushiku (Ushiku, Ibaraki Prefecture)

2002 House in Karuizawa (Karuizawa, Nagano Prefecture)

2003 House in Zushi (Zushi, Kanagawa Prefecture)

Apartment in Tamagawa Denen-chofu (Setagaya-ku, Tokyo)

2004 House in Fuchu (Fuchu-shi, Tokyo)

House in Yuigahama (Kamakura, Kanagawa Prefecture)

House in Sakurayama (Zushi, Kanagawa Prefecture)

House in Kamakurayama (Kamakura, Kanagawa Prefecture)

2005 House in Kamakurayama (Kamakura, Kanagawa Prefecture)

6. Imoto Shigemi

office Imoto Architects

2-17-10-201 Minato, Chuo-ku, Fukuoka 810-0075, Fukuoka Prefecture

phone/fax +81 92 715 1012/+81 92 715 1036

email/url imoto@alpha.ocn.ne.jp/www11.ocn.ne.jp/~imoto/

selected projects

Sun Terrace Imajuku (Nishi-ku, Fukuoka)

J House (Chuo-ku, Fukuoka)

1996 Gakuan (Chikushino, Fukuoka Prefecture)

1999 Shima Residence (Shima, Fukuoka Prefecture)

2001 Tani Villa (Chuo-ku, Fukuoka)

2004 M Residence (Nijo, Fukuoka Prefecture)

Yufuin Residence (Yufuin, Oita Prefecture)

K House (Higashi-ku, Fukuoka)

H House (Ogoori, Fukuoka Prefecture)

2005　K House (Higashi-ku, Fukuoka)

2006　H House (Ogoori, Fukuoka Prefecture)

7. Ishii Daigo

office Ishii Daigo+ Future-scape Architects

Yahagi Building 401, 1-19-14 Yoyogi, Shibuya-ku, Tokyo 151-0053

phone/fax +81 3 5350 0855 / +81 3 5350 0854

e-mail/url info@future-scape.co.jp / http://www.future-scape.co.jp/

selected projects

1994　Circulation (Kashiwa, Chiba Prefecture)

1997　White Blue Black (Mitaka-shi, Tokyo)

2000　Cottage in Tsumari (Tokamachi, Niigata Prefecture)

House of Light (Tokamachi, Niigata Prefecture)

2002　Restaurant Suzaku-Mon (Itabashi-ku, Tokyo)

House in Aihra (Machida-shi, Tokyo)

2003　House in Meguro (Meguro-ku, Tokyo)

2004　House Facing Cherry Trees (Koganei-shi, Tokyo)

2005　Tendo PLY (Meguro-ku, Tokyo)

2006　Annex of An Old House (Akiruno-shi, Tokyo)

8. Ishii Hideki

office Ishii Hideki Architect Atelier

2F 1-5-24 Suido, Bunkyo-ku, Tokyo 112-0005

phonel/fax +81 3 3818 1172/+81 3 3818 1173

email/url info@isi-arch.com/www.isi-arch.com

selected projects

1998　Nagareru Mori no Michi (Kumagaya, Saitama Prefecture)

2002　T2 (Kawasaki City)

2003　S2 (Kawasaki City)

ONOF (Yokohama City)

2004　CRES (Kawasaki City)

2005　Shin Yokohama House (Yokohama City)

2006　Miyamaedaira House (Kawasaki City)

Mitusawa House (Yokohama City)

2007　Kajigaya House (Kawasaki City)

F-flat (Kawasaki City)

9. Izumi Masatoshi+Yamamoto Tadashi

office Izumi Stone Works

3524-10 Mure, Mure-cho, Kita-gun, Kagawa Prefecture 761-0121

phone/fax +81 87 870 1600/ +81 87 845 6777

url www.izumi-stoneworks.com

10. Kimura Hiroaki

office Kimura Hiroaki+Ks Architects & Associates

309 Ohe Building, 2-8-1, Nishitenma, Kita-ku, Osaka 530-0047

phone/fax +81 6 6365 6536 /+81 6 6365 6065

e-mail/url kimura@ks-architects.com/www.ks-architects.com

selected projects

1990　U.S. FLAT (Osaka Prefecture)

House of Labyrinth (Hyogo Prefecture)

Common City Hoshida Community Center (Osaka Prefecture)

A House (Wakayama Prefecture)

3 in1 House (Hyogo Prefecture)

N's ARK (Hyogo Prefecture)

1/4 Circle (Hyogo Prefecture)

2000　Ta House (Kobe City)

Sa House (Shiga Prefecture)

Osaka Architectural Competition Governor's Award for 4 in 1

Mo House (Kobe City)

2004　Kobe Shichiya Hall (Kobe City)

Steel Sheet Farmhouse & Teahouse (Osaka Prefecture)

Kobe City Environmental Point Award for Kobe Shichiya Hall

2005　Kobe Shinsei Baptist Church (Kobe City)

JIA Kansai Architects Award, Grand Prize

2006　Tower House (Shiga Prefecture)

11. Kobayashi Hisashi

office Kobayashi Hisashi Architect & Associates, Inc.

16-18-001 Kusunoki-cho Ashiya, Hyogo Prefecture 659-0015

phone/fax +81 797 38 0789 / +81 797 38 0783

e-mail cova24h@world.ocn.ne.jp

selected projects

1984　Court House at Higashi Sumiyoshi (Higashi Sumiyoshi-ku, Osaka)

1984　Ashiya Flats (Ashiya, Hyogo Prefecture)

1987　Shoe Gallery Ota (Ashiya, Hyogo Prefecture)

1991　Sakurajosui Studio (Setagaya-ku, Tokyo)

1994　White Magnolia (Kobe City)

1998　House at Megamiyama (Nishinomiya, Hyogo Prefecture)

1998　G-Cube (Kobe City)

1998　Sunny Hill West (Ashiya, Hyogo Prefecture)

1999　House at Iwazono (Ashiya, Hyogo Prefecture)

2001　House at Hiraisansoh (Takarazuka, Hyogo Prefecture)

2004　Muragen (Arima, Hyogo Prefecture)

2006　Le Toa Beauty School (Tennoji-ku, Osaka)

2007　Muragen (Ashiya, Hyogo Prefecture)

12. Kosugi Hirohisa

office Prop Position

#202 Meguro House 2-10-22 Mita, Meguro-ku, Tokyo 153-0062

phone/fax +81 3 3760 8299/+81 3 3760 8298

email/url prop@crocus.ocn.ne.jp/ www.prop-position.co.jp

selected projects

1999　J2 Complex Office (Chuo-ku, Tokyo)

2000　K-Factory (Kuwana, Mie Prefecture)

2006　AAC CLINIC GINZA (Chuo-ku, Tokyo)

2007　Karuizawa -A2 (Karuizawa, Nagano Prefecture)

Karuizawa –K (Karuizawa, Nagano Prefecture)

AAC CLINIC NAGOYA (Nagoya City)

House-IS (Nagoya City)

Karuizawa-OH (Karuizawa, Nagano Prefecture)

House-DC (Ohta-ku, Tokyo)

13. Mori Kiyotoshi+Kawamura Natsuko

office MDS Studio

5-8-6-502 Yoyogi, Shibuya-ku, Tokyo

phone/ fax +81 3 3465 6648/+81 3 5941 8590

e-mail/url info@mds-arch.com/www.mds-arch.com

selected projects/awards

2002 Oji Timber Head Office (Koto-ku, Tokyo)

2003 Good Design Award

2004 American Wood Design Award

2005 House in Kakamigahara (Kakamigahara, Gifu Prefecture)

2006 JID (Japan Interior Designer's Association) Award

House in Saginuma (Kawasaki, Kanagawa Prefecture)

2007 House in Minamiaoyama (Minato-ku, Tokyo)

House in Azamino (Aoba-ku, Yokohama)

14. Nakagame Kiyonobu

office Nakagame Kiyonobu Architect and Associates

1-11-1 B1 Shishigaya Tsurumi-ku Yokohama 230-0073, Kanagawa Prefecture

phone/fax +81 45 581 9812

email/url info@nakagame.com/ www.nakagame.com

selected projects

2004 House in Toyooka (Tsurumi-ku, Yokohama)

2005 House in Futamatagawa (Asahi-ku, Yokohama)

House in Nakadai-2 (Tsurumi-ku, Yokohama)

2006 House in Kasumi (Narashino, Chiba Prefecture)

House in Kichijoji (Mitaka-shi, Tokyo)

House in Izumichuo (Izumi-ku, Yokohama)

2007 Townhouse in Narita (Narita, Chiba Prefecture)

House in Minamiboso (Minamiboso, Chiba Prefecture)

15. Nakahara Yuji

office Nakahara Yuji Architect Design Office

2F Nakahara Bldg. 1-19-19 Arata, Kagoshima 890-0054, Kagoshima Prefecture

phone/fax +81 99 256 1911/+81 99 256 1051

email/url info@ yn-architect.co.jp /www.yn-architect.co.jp

selected projects

1994 F Residence (Ijuin, Kagoshima prefecture)

House in Myoenji (Ijuin, Kagoshima Prefecture)

1997 Scene House in Sakurajima (Kagoshima City)

1999 House in Kagoshima (Kagoshima City)

2001 House in Shimoarata (Shimoarata, Kagoshima Prefecture)

Courthouse in Jinganji (Jiganji, Kagoshima Prefecture)

Float Box (Kagoshima City)

House in Yoshino (Yoshino, Kagoshima Prefecture)

2005 Sky House (Kagoshima City)

2006 House in Harara (Kagoshima City)

2007 A Residence (Kagoshima City)

16. Nakazono Tetsuya

office naf architect and design

#203, 8-12 Nishihiratsuka-cho, Naka-ku, Hiroshima 730-0024 Hiroshima Prefecture

phone/fax +81 82 543 4602 /+81 82 543 4603

e-mail/url hiroshima@naf-add.com/www.naf-aad.com

selected projects/awards

2000 Bistro & Bar Toya (Higashi Hiroshima City)

Shuho Sugii (Higashi Hiroshima City)

2001 Kusunokusu Shops (Hiroshima City and Fukuoka City)

2002 Bar Kurato (Higashi Hiroshima City)

2003 Bar Kobiki (Yoshidacho, Hiroshima Prefecture)

Kai House (Hiroshima City)

Green Bank (Kure City, Hiroshima Prefecture)

2004 Tapiau (Singal, Korea)

2005 Flat Form (Higashi Hiroshima City)

Slate House (Hiroshima City)

Good Design Award Architectural and Design Division

2006 JIA (Japan Institute of Architects) Award

Bucharest Architectural Biennale

17. Niizeki Kenichiro

office Niizeki Studio

2-12-3-402 Kichijoji- Honcho, Musashino-shi, Tokyo 180-0004

phone/fax +81 422 22 2110/+81 422 22 4110

email/url studio@niizekistudio.com/www.niizekistudio.com

selected projects

1997 House in Shoan (Tokyo)

1998 Garden in Zoshigaya (Toshima-ku,Tokyo)

1999 Showroom in Kichijoji (Kichijoji-shi, Tokyo)

2000 Gallery in Shibuya (Shibuya-ku, Tokyo)

House in Yoyogi (Shibuya-ku, Tokyo)

2001 House in Atami (Shizuoka Prefecture)

Park in Musashino (Musashino-shi, Tokyo)

2002 House in Hiroo (Shibuya-ku, Tokyo)

Grave in Obadai (Chiba Prefecture)

2003 House in Yachimata (Chiba Prefecture)

House in Nakamichi Kichijoji-shi, Tokyo)

2004 House in Araiyakushi (Nakano-ku, Tokyo)

House in Sakunoyama (Aichi Prefecture)

2005 House in Kamogawa (Chiba Prefecture)

Shop in Shibuya (Shibuya-ku, Tokyo)

2006 House in Yoyogiuehara (Shibuya-ku,Tokyo)

18. Ogawa Shinichi

office Ogawa Shinichi & Associates

5-33-18 Inokuchi, Nishi-ku, Hiroshima 733-0842, Hiroshima Prefecture

phone/fax +81 82 278 7099 /+81 82 278 7107

e-mail/url info@shinichiogawa.com/www.shinichiogawa.com

selected projects

1998 White Cube (Hiroshima City)

1999 Cassina ixc. Hiroshima (Hiroshima City)

2001 Tunnel House (Hiroshima City)

2002 Barbas (Yamaguchi City)

104X (Yamaguchi City)

Abstract House (Onomichi, Hiroshima Prefecture)

2003 K House (Tokyo)

2004 Court House (Saitama Prefecture)

Loft House (Nagoya City)

Twincourt House (Fukuoka Prefecture)

2007 World of Calvin Klein / THE HOUSE (Tokyo)

36m House (Kagawa Prefecture)

White Court House (Tokyo)

K House (Tokyo)

Void House (Gifu Prefecture)

19. Oshio Shoji

office UA Architects Tokyo office

5-12-6-3F Kita-shinagawa Shinagawa-ku, Tokyo 141-0001

phone/fax +81 3 5421 7188+81 3 5421 3622

email/url tokyo@ua-office.co.jp/ www.ua-office.co.jp

selected projects

2003 House in Fujimigaoka (Utsunomiya, Tochigi Prefecture)

2004 Bistro La Mariejeanne (Chuo-ku, Tokyo)

House in Shimotamachi (Kanuma, Tochigi Prefecture)

House in Hiramatsuhoncho (Utsunomiya, Tochigi Prefecture)

House O (Koganei-shi, Tokyo)

2006 Light Gallery (Tachikawa, Tokyo)

Interaction Gallery (Tachikawa, Tokyo)

fu-house (Setagaya-ku ,Tokyo)

2007 House in Nishiosakabe (Utsunomiya, Tochigi Prefecture)

20. Saitoh Yoshihiro

office A-study Co. Ltd.

4F Tak Bldg. 6-13-14 Minami-ooi, Shinagawa-ku, Tokyo 140-0013

phone/fax +81-3-5767-6146/+81-3-5767-6156

email/url info@a-study.jp /www.a-study.jp

selected projects

2004 Rise (Nakano, Nagano Prefecture)

2005 M-House (Souka, Saitama Prefecture)

N-House (Matsushiro-cho, Nagano Prefecture)

N-Clinic (Tsuzuki-ku, Kanagawa Prefecture)

2006 Jewelry Shop Itoi (Oota, Gunma Prefecture)

21. Suzuki Edward

office Edward Suzuki Associates

Keyaki House 101, 19-10, 3-chome Nishi-Azabu, Minato-ku, Tokyo 106-0031

phone/fax +81 3 5770 5395/ +81 3 5770-5397

email/url esa@edward.net /www.edward.net

selected projects

1985 Udagawa-cho Police Box (Shibuya-ku, Tokyo)

Nishimachi International School (Minato-ku, Tokyo)

1986 Onward Daikanyama Bldg. (Shibuya-ku, Tokyo)

1988 Shizuoka gas S gee Port (Shimizu, Shizuoka, Prefecture)

1990 Joule-A (Minato-ku, Tokyo)

1992 Mpata Lodge, Safari Park Hotel (Kenya)

1993 Japan Railway East Akayu Station (Yamagata, Prefecture)

1995 Musicasa (Shibuya-ku, Tokyo)

1996 Library for the Blind (Shinjuku-ku, Tokyo)

1997 Japan Railway East Ohmagari Station (Akita Prefecture)

2000 Japan Railway East Shin-Toshin Station (Ohmiya City, Tokyo)

2001 Y Residence and Guesthouse (Shibuya-ku, Tokyo)

2002 Shisui Parking Area Service Facilities (Chiba Prefecture)

2003 Gamo Beauty Salon (Minato-ku, Tokyo)

22. Takayasu Shigekazu+Imazu Shuhei

office Architecture Lab

2F 2-13-3 Kaminarimon, Taito-ku, Tokyo 111-0034

phone/fax +81 3 3845 7320 fax +81 3 3845 7352

e-mail/url takayasu@architecture-lab.com/ www.architecture-lab.com

selected projects

1997 Kazu Dental Clinic (Kamisu, Ibaraki Prefecture)

1998 Storage Core House (Sumida-ku, Tokyo)

2001 Kawaguchi Intersection Housing (Kawaguchi, Saitama Prefecture)

2002 Nerima H House (Nerima-ku, Tokyo)

White Box House (Itabashi-ku, Tokyo)

2003 Misumi Residence (Tsukubamirai, Ibaraki Prefecture)

Patch House (Kamakura, Kanagawa Prefecture)

2004 Fujimi Kindergarden (Funabashi, Chiba Prefecture)

2005 Tokyo University of Science, Communication Dept. (Noda, Chiba Prefecture)

Narihira (Sumida-ku, Tokyo)

2006 Nina Dental Clinic (Yatsushiro, Kumamoto Prefecture)

23. Takei Makoto+Nabeshima Chie

office TNA (Takei Nabeshima Architects)

5-10-19-3F Yagumo, Meguro-ku, Tokyo 152-0023

phone/fax +81 3 5701 1901/+81 3 5701 1902

e-mail/url mail@tna-arch.com/www.tna-arch.com

selected projects

2005 Wood Wear House (Hayama, Kanagawa Prefecture)

Color Concrete House (Yokohama, Kanagawa Prefecture)

2007 Wood Ship Café (Hayama, Kanagawa Prefecture)

Mosaic House (Meguro-ku, Tokyo)

24. Tanijiri Makoto

office Suppose Design Office

13-2 Kako-machi, Naka-ku, Hiroshima 730-0812

phone/fax +81 82 247 1152/+81 82 247 1152

email/url info@suppose.jp/www.suppose.jp

selected projects

2003 Bishamon House (Asaminami-ku, Hiroshima)

Misonou House (Higashi Hiroshima City)

2004 Kuchita Building (Kita-ku, Hiroshima)

Kameyama House (Asakita-ku, Hiroshima)

Ushitashinmachi House (Higashi-ku, Hiroshima)

Ohno House (Ohno-cho, Hiroshima)

20005 Kurume House (Kurume, Fukuoka Prefecture)

2006 House in Hiratsuka (Hiratsuka, Kanagawa Prefecture)

Kannabe House (Fukuyama, Hiroshima Prefecture)

Minamimachi House (Minami-ku, Hiroshima)

2007 Wakayama House (Wakayama City)

Kure House (Kure, Hiroshima Prefecture)

Koufu House (Kai, Yamanashi Prefecture)

Sumiyoshi House (Naka-ku, Hiroshima)

Gouhara House (Kure, Hiroshima Prefecture)

25. Utsumi Tomoyuki

office Milligram Architectural Studio
4-2-17 Kugahara, Ota-ku, Tokyo, 146-0085
phone/fax +81 3 5700 8155/+81 3 5700 8156
email/url info@milligram.ne.jp/www.milligram.ne.jp

selected projects

2000 House in Nakaikegami (Ota-ku, Tokyo)
2001 House in Kawana (Kawana, Shizuoka Prefecture)
Inner Skin House (Shibuya-ku, Tokyo)
2002 House in Hiroo (Minato-ku, Tokyo)
Studio Flat & Passage (Minato-ku, Tokyo)
2003 Assortment House (Minato-ku, Tokyo)
Turret (Shibuya-ku, Tokyo)
2004 Towered Flats (Kita-ku, Tokyo)
Forest of Steel (Nakano-ku, Tokyo)
Tavola (Saitama City)
Arc-Shaped Extension (Karuizawa, Nagano Prefecture)
2005 C-1 (Shibuya-ku, Tokyo)
Suit G (Ota-ku, Tokyo)
2006 Nestled Box (Chofu-shi, Tokyo)

26. Watanabe Akira

office Watanabe Akira Architect and Associates
4-16-19 Meguro-ku Tokyo Japan 152-0003
phone/fax +81 3 3710 1963/+81 3 3710 1872
email/url awaas@tky3.3web.ne.jp/http://www2.tky.3web.ne.jp/~awaas/

selected projects

1986 Niki Club Phase 1 (Nasu City, Tochigi Prefecture)
1991 Sapporo Hiroshima Prince Hotel (Sapporo, Hokkaido Prefecture)
Camellia House (Wakayama Prefecture)
House in Seijo (Setagaya-ku, Tokyo)
1996 House in Seijo (Setagaya-ku, Tokyo)
Hyoseki-kaku Inn (Hakone City, Kanagawa Prefecture)
1997 Niki Club Phase 2 (Nasu City, Tochigi Prefecture)
House in Setagaya (Setagaya-ku, Tokyo)
House in Mejiro-dai (Bunkyo-ku, Tokyo)
1998 Saita Memorial Museum (Setagaya-ku, Tokyo)
2000 W HOUSE (Meguro-ku, Tokyo)
2002 House in Kamisuwa (Kamisuwa, Nagano Prefecture)
2003 Rakuyoso Inn (Sakyo-ku, Kyoto)
2005 Public Restroom in Hasuike Moat (Chiyoda-ku, Tokyo)
House in Seijo (Setagaya-ku, Tokyo)
2006 House in Shiroganedai (Minato-ku,Tokyo)

27. Yagi Masashi+Yagi Konomi

office Yagi Architectural Design
5-9-14 Hisagi, Zushi-shi, Kanagawa Prefecture 249-0001
phone/fax +81 46 870 6604/+81 46 870 6605
email/url yagi@zj9.so-net.ne.jp/www.yagi-arc.com

selected projects

2003 Nojiriko Villa (Shinano-machi, Nagano Prefecture)
2004 Tamagawa Denenchofu Residence Remodel (Setagaya-ku, Tokyo)